DANIEL KLEIN
BLUE SUEDE CLUES

Daniel Martin Klein is an American writer of fiction, non-fiction, and humor. After majoring in philosophy at Harvard, and a brief career in television comedy, he began writing books, ranging from thrillers and mysteries to humorous books about philosophy. These include the *New York Times* bestseller *Plato and a Platypus Walk Into a Bar: Understanding Philosophy Through Jokes* (with Thomas Cathcart), and the *Sunday Times* bestseller *Travels With Epicurus*.

The four Elvis Mysteries were originally published in the early 2000s to great critical and commercial acclaim.

DANIEL KLEIN

BLUE SUEDE CLUES

DEAN STREET PRESS

For Tom & Eloise

Acknowledgments

THANKS to my daughter, Samara, my wife, Freke, and my pal Tom for reading and criticizing the first draft of this little opus. I am also indebted to those uncanny Elvis mavens who wish to be known publicly as simply the ElvisNews.com team editors, and Elvis expert par excellence David Neale, editor of *Elvis in Print*, for checking succeeding drafts for accuracy (and man, did they catch some whoppers!). Thank you all.

Many thanks also to Doug Ferguson, who guided me through some intricacies of California law in the 1960s.

As always, I am deeply indebted to the work of Peter Guralnick, whose two-volume biography of The King, *Last Train to Memphis* and *Careless Love*, and his more recent book, *Elvis, Day by Day* (with Ernst Jorgensen), are required reading for anyone who wants to grasp the real Elvis.

Finally, thanks again to my agent, Howard Morhaim, who led me to this series, to my editors and shepherds at St. Martin's Press, Charlie Spicer and Joe Cleemann, and to the director Barnet Kellman, who instantly saw the filmic possibilities of this series. I shall not want.

D. M. K.

PROLOGUE

ON THE day that Holly McDougal was strangled to death on the MGM lot in Hollywood, Elvis Presley was in Nashville pulling an all-nighter with the Jordanaires and the A-list of local studio musicians. It was Elvis's first recording session since returning from the army, and the album that came out of it—*Elvis Is Back*—produced the hit single "Fame and Fortune."

The McDougal homicide and the trial that followed never made it into a single newspaper east of the Rockies. Holly McDougal was, after all, just a bit player murdered by a nobody.

1
SETTING THE STORY STRAIGHT

November 1963

ELVIS took a flying leap over a hay bale, executed a lackluster hip twitch in mid-air, and landed ungracefully on his heels. Behind the camera, Gene Nelson, the director, was making monkey faces at him and mouthing the word, "Smile." Elvis cranked up the corners of his mouth like he was hauling dead weights out of the sea.

"Cut!" Nelson shouted.

The playback stopped and the entire cast of *Kissin' Cousins* stumbled to a halt. Nelson ambled over to Elvis with a pleading look in his pale gray eyes.

"*Please*, Elvis, it's the last day," Nelson said soothingly. "Try and look like you're having fun."

"I ain't *that* good an actor," Elvis replied, deadpan.

Fact was, it had taken a supreme act of willpower for Elvis to drag himself onto the MGM lot that morning to finish filling in the dance sequences. He'd been able to overlook just how ridiculous this picture was while they were on location, up in the luminous San Bernadino Mountains, but back here, hearing himself sing those godawful hillbilly songs in playback, there was no way he could ignore how moronic it was.

"Well, *I'm* having fun," Wayne LeFevre said, sidling up beside Elvis with a goofy grin. "Just pretend you're me, Elvis."

LeFevre was Elvis's double. Elvis played two roles in *Cousins*: Jodie Tatum, a dim-witted yokel straight out of *L'il Abner*, and Josh Morgan, Tatum's straight-arrow, Army lieutenant, look-alike cousin. When both cousins appeared in a scene—like in this hoedown number—LeFevre stood in for one of them.

"Man, you'd have fun at a public hanging," Elvis muttered to LeFevre.

"At least I'd try to make myself useful—like by comforting the widow in my own obliging way," LeFevre replied, winking.

"One more time!" Nelson called out. "Hit your marks, folks!"

Elvis rambled back to the hay bale, hooked a thumb into the pocket of his Josh Morgan army khakis, and was preparing to leap on the downbeat when he spotted Colonel Parker galloping onto the set. The Colonel's bovine face was a mean shade of red. A newspaper flapped in his stubby right hand.

"Time-out!" Parker hollered, and Nelson flashed five fingers for a five-minute break.

"Son, we are thigh deep in cow patties this time," Parker said, thrusting the newspaper in front of Elvis's face.

Elvis peered down at it. The headline read "Elvis Wins Love of Ann-Margret." It was datelined London, where Miss Ann was attending the royal premiere of *Bye Bye Birdie* and where she had taken it upon herself to announce to the press that she and Elvis were in love, adding, "I cannot say when, or if, we will marry."

"Fool woman," Elvis mumbled, even as a genuine smiled tugged at the corners of his mouth.

"Damn shot worse than a fool," Parker snapped. "That woman's a home wrecker."

God Almighty, the Colonel was right. Elvis hadn't figured that when Miss Priscilla saw this—and some damned fool would surely show it to her—she'd throw a fit and a half. She'd just flown in from Memphis day before yesterday with a bad case of jealousy on the brain, and this could put her over the top. Make her threaten to go running home to Daddy in Germany again.

"Guess we need to do something about this," Elvis murmured.

"I'm doing it already," Parker snapped. "Called a press conference for six sharp. We'll set the story straight."

Elvis watched the Colonel greet the reporters at his MGM office door, where he was decked out in knickers, a buttoned-up Hawaiian shirt, a floppy bow tie and, to top it off, Elvis's *Kissin' Cousins* blond wig set at a jaunty angle on his moon-shaped head. It was one of the Colonel's standard gambits: When you've got a crisis, bamboozle them with buffoonery. After the journalists had taken their seats, he grinned at them for a full minute, then removed the cigar from his mouth and barked, "Okay, gents, one question per. And be gentle, boys, Mr. Presley has been feeling kind of put upon lately."

Elvis lowered his eyes. The way Parker put things, Elvis always ended up sounding like some touchy mamma's boy.

The first question came from Dunlap of the *Hollywood Reporter*. "Exactly how would you describe your relationship with Ann-Margret?"

Elvis leaned back in the Colonel's leather desk chair and scratched his jaw. He was still in costume and makeup, so his fingernails scraped off a thin line of tan foundation. "I would describe our relationship as a deep friendship," Elvis began. "Sort of like brother and sister. Yes, Miss Ann is like my long-lost sister."

Truth to tell, he *had* felt a deep connection to his *Viva Las Vegas* co-star the moment he laid eyes on her. And that connection went way beyond Ann-Margret's sexy good looks. He'd felt from the start that she was a soul mate, some kind of female mirror image of himself.

"So you are denying that there is anything romantic going on between the two of you?" the *Variety* reporter said.

Elvis sat up straight and looked directly in the reporter's eyes. "Sir, *denying* and *affirming* are awful grand words to be using when you're talking about romance. Seem more like church words, if you know what I mean."

From the corner of his eye, Elvis saw the Colonel grinning and nodding with approval. No doubt he thought Elvis was doing a little bamboozle of his own, but actually Elvis was trying to get a point across, so he went on. "You see, there are all kinds of ways that a man and a woman connect with one another and most of them are a mystery. Least they are to me. So it's hard to put into words exactly the way I feel about Miss Ann. It's a deep and complicated feeling."

The Colonel turned to Elvis and pumped his eyebrows up and down by way of reproach; this wasn't going the way he'd scripted it.

Ferguson from *Time* magazine chimed in with: "With all due respect, Mr. Presley, you've been seen all over town motorcycling with Miss Margret, holding hands, going into your trailer with her and closing the door behind you . . ."

In spite of himself, Elvis felt the sweetness of those glorious times with Ann-Margret sweep over him. The feeling only lasted a split second, but that was long enough to show in his eyes; the reporters responded with knowing smiles and started scratching furiously in their notepads.

That did it; this was going from bad to worse. The Colonel popped in front of Elvis. "Thank you, gentlemen," he said dismissively. "I know you'll do right by Mr. Presley in your papers. Now we've got stills from our new movie over on the table there. You can pick them up on your way out."

"One last question please, Elvis." It was Mike Murphy, the famously wise-guy reporter from the *L.A. Times*. "And I promise you, it's got nothing to do with your private life."

The Colonel started to wave him off, but Elvis stood and said, "Okay, one last one."

"Well, I was talking with Hal Wallis the other day," Murphy began, "and he said that he just *loves* producing your pictures, because with all the money he makes from them, he gets to make first-rate films with actors like Richard Burton and Peter O'Toole. Would you care to comment on that?"

It felt like a punch in the gut. Elvis reeled back into his chair. That one hurt bad, terrible bad. Far worse than anything anybody could say about his love life. No, this one got Elvis right where he lived. His great pal Hal Wallis had put it out there plain and simple: Elvis was just a money machine so Wallis could make *real* movies, movies that actually meant something, unlike this joke of a picture. And damnit, the Colonel had handpicked *Kissin' Cousins*. He'd said the script had *Elvis* written all over it.

The Colonel shot eye daggers at Murphy. He yanked the blond wig off his head in what he must have thought was a gesture of fury, but it only made him look more buffoonish. Man, Elvis hated that wig. He'd hated it every time he had to put it on to play that pea-brained country bumpkin, Jodie Tatum. And at this moment, he hated it with all his heart because he saw it for it what it really was—a clown's wig. And *he* was the clown.

Before the Colonel could say another word, Elvis rose again from his chair. If he had been shaky on his feet a moment before, he was steady as a rock now. He stood tall and calm and resolute in his army khakis with the lieutenant's stripes, looking for all the world like a man in command. The entire room went dead quiet, a couple of the reporters freezing in mid-motion as they packed up their notebooks and pens.

"Let me put something straight here," Elvis began in a low voice. "There is nothing I would like to do more than make a picture that has some real meaning to it. A picture that would give folks something to think about after they left the movie theater. Something to consider about their own lives. Maybe about their families or their country or anything else that's meaningful to them."

Elvis paused, looking the reporters in the eye one at a time. He felt better than he had all day and he surely knew why: He was finally speaking his own lines.

"I'm no great actor," he went on. "No Richard Burton or Peter O'Toole. I wouldn't kid myself about something like that. But that doesn't mean I couldn't do a real picture if I had the right script. And that's the thing I want to say here. I want to find a story—a movie story—that I'd be proud to make. I don't know what that would be, but I'm pretty sure I'd know it if I read it. So I'd appreciate it if you gentlemen would do me the favor of writing in your papers that I am on the lookout for a first-class script. I don't care who writes it. Could be a fisherman or a truck driver for all

I know. But I'm looking. And I need your help finding it. Thank you. Thank you very much."

The reporters broke into spontaneous applause. In the doorway, Ned Florbid, the sleek MGM production manager who had wandered in during Elvis's little speech, joined the applause, smiling broadly. And then Colonel Parker started clapping too, the blond wig swinging comically from one hand, but clapping for all he was worth. That was one of his standard gambits too: Always cheer, but cheer the loudest when you are losing.

2
SILENT NIGHT

THE reporters had been gone for several minutes before either Elvis or the Colonel said a word. Then, without looking at Elvis, Parker pointed his cigar to a corner of his office.

"You want to read scripts?" he intoned. "Well, I got a whole crate of 'em right over there. And that's just last week's. That should keep you busy for a while, son."

Parker stuck the cigar back in his mouth and stalked out of his office.

Elvis walked slowly to the picture window overlooking the MGM lot. It was dusk, but there was still plenty of activity out there. Two guys in cowboy outfits sauntered by eating hot dogs. A mini tractor swung around them, towing a calliope on a flat bed. Standing in front of the door to Sound Studio C, a statuesque blonde puffed furiously on a cigarette; all she was wearing was a silk dressing gown that didn't quite cover her buttocks.

That feeling of steady calm that had come over Elvis when he spoke his desire to make a meaningful movie was already ebbing away. Up and down, back and forth, around and around—seems he couldn't hold on to any one feeling for longer than a minute. All his hankerings seemed to come in opposites these days. Like Ann-Margret and Priscilla. Those two couldn't be more different from one another, but each one seemed like the perfect woman when he was with the *other* one. Same for Graceland and his house in Bel Air. When he was in Graceland, he felt all cooped up, especially now that Dad and that woman, Dee, had taken up residence. Still, not a day went by out here when he didn't find himself hurting for home. It even went for the Colonel. One minute he'd be thanking his lucky stars for sending him Colonel Tom Parker to lead the way on this fabulous joyride. And the next minute he'd be cursing the day he met Parker, reviling him for dragging him further and further away from the life and the music that were in his soul.

Elvis turned from the window and ambled over to the corner where the Colonel had pointed. As promised, a wooden peach crate sat there piled high with faux leather-bound movie scripts. He picked up the top one, brought it to Parker's desk, and pulled the chain on the banker's lamp. The title was *Flubber Rock* by one Richard Persky.

> FADE IN:
> Long Shot of 16-foot Chris-Craft bobbing in open sea. Gulf of Mexico. Two figures, a MAN and a WOMAN, both in bathing suits and snorkeling gear, dive off the side.
> Medium Shot as CAMERA descends underwater with them. We see the MAN (Mr. Presley) and the WOMAN (Tuesday Weld? Ann-Margret?) facing each other, bubbles emerging from their snorkel tubes. They are SINGING.
> SONG: "Bubbling with Love"

Elvis closed the script right there and pushed it to the corner of the desk. He went back to the peach crate, hunkered down, and pulled the next script off the pile, *Pickles and Cream* by Bruce Person. He opened to the first page, still crouching.

> FADE IN:
> Long Shot of Drugstore. Through the window, we see a long soda fountain, every stool occupied by a PRETTY YOUNG WOMAN, and behind the counter, a HANDSOME YOUNG MAN (Mr. Presley), is making an ice cream soda.

As the CAMERA MOVES INSIDE we hear the HYM SINGING.

SONG: "Two Scoops of Love."

Elvis dropped the script back onto the pile. *Damnation!* Maybe he should stop making movies altogether and get back to just recording songs. *Real* songs, not cornball movie ditties with cornball titles like those groaners from *Kissin' Cousins*: "Barefoot Ballad," my foot! And "One Boy, Two Little Girls"—that one sounded like a nursery rhyme for slow learners. Those songs were about as authentic as Mountain Dew pop since they sold out to Pepsi. Worse. Coming as they did out of the Hollywood song mill, they had a built-in wink to show that these Tinseltown songwriters were superior to the songs they churned out. And surely to show that they were superior to the man who would sing them. Fact was, these Hollywood types couldn't write a genuine song—a song with a true heart and soul like "It's Now or Never"—if their lives depended on it.

Elvis was just straightening up when he saw the photograph lying in the Colonel's wastebasket. It was a photo of Elvis in an army uniform—a *real* army uniform—with a guitar in his hands, and it looked like he was singing. Other soldiers all around him. And something—a tree?—just behind him. Strange. He hadn't given any public performances while he was in the army. That was part of the deal: He'd insisted on being treated like any other private and that meant no performing, not even for the troops.

He picked the photograph out of the wastebasket and held it under the desk lamp. That *was* a tree behind him, a Christmas tree. Suddenly, it came back to him—Christmas Day, four long years ago, in Friedberg, Germany. He and his company had set up a Christmas party for a nearby orphanage, then returned to Ray Kaserne and decided to decorate their home away from home for the holidays. When they'd finished, one of the guys had brought out a guitar and started singing "The First Noel." Pretty soon, everyone was singing "Jingle Bells" and "Santa Claus Is Coming to Town" and "God Rest Ye Merry Gentlemen." Elvis was singing along too and at one point the guy handed the guitar off to him.

They all kept singing until they got to "Silent Night" and then, one by one, the others dropped out, leaving Elvis to sing it solo. And sing he did, poured his heart into it for all the Christmas trees and Christmas dinners every one of his comrades would be missing that year. It had come out of him all gospel, the song singing itself. At one point, the guys with weekend passes started to file out and, when they passed by Elvis as he sang, they just touched his sleeve and continued to the door, not saying a word. When he came to the end with a soaring, "Sleep in heavenly peace," no one clapped or cheered. They just stood there, silently happy and sad and grateful. Finally, Elvis had called out, "Merry Christmas, everyone" and they'd called back, "Merry Christmas, Elvis." Elvis remembered thinking then, as he thought again now: *That* is why I sing. That's what it's all about, right there.

Elvis saw that there was a faint pencil line circling the head of one of the soldiers at the edge of the photo and next to it the word "me." He leaned his head closer. It was a baby-faced soldier with sleepy eyes and a loopy smile. Elvis had no idea who he was. Just another GI keeping up a brave face far from home. But why had he sent the photo? And why the heck was the Colonel throwing it out without showing it to him first? Colonel knew this was just the kind of photograph that Elvis saved for his personal photo album.

Elvis walked back to the wastepaper basket and squatted next to it. It stank of cigars and spit and fermenting pizza crusts. He poked around with one finger. Another photo, this one of a pretty young woman with bare shoulders and short curly hair. It had writing on it too in ink: "Elvis, I'll do anything you want me to. ANYTHING! I love you, Doris Frimel. Telephone 555-3298." That's what passed for fan mail these days. Elvis pushed it off to the side next to a cigar stub. And there he saw a crimped-up piece of blue-lined notebook paper with something written on it in pencil. He brought it back to the desk and ironed it flat with his fist.

Dear Mr. Presley,

No reason for you to remember me, but this little photograph holds one of the happiest memories of my young life. It's a memory of a Christmas carol that raised up my spirits at a time when they were kind of sagging.

Let me be honest with you, Mr. Presley, I'm just another guy down on his luck who is reaching out to you. I bet you get letters like this all the time, so I wouldn't be surprised if you just crumpled this up and threw it away along about right now.

Elvis smiled to himself—Colonel had already taken care of that part. He read on:

Thing is, I'm in prison, California Correctional Institution up in Tehachapi, and I'm not just doing time, I'm doing the rest of my life. Murder, first degree, of a young girl. But you see, I didn't do it. I swear I didn't on the grave of my mother, Agnes P. Littlejon, may she rest in peace.

So here goes: I need someone to stand up for me. Stand up and prove they got the wrong man. It's gotta be somebody folks would really listen to. And you're the only person in the world I ever met who fits that bill. You don't owe me nothing, Mr. Presley, I know that. I'm just asking.

Gratefully yours for that long ago "Silent Night,"
Freddy "Squirm" Littlejon

Elvis looked again at the photograph. No, he didn't remember Squirm Littlejon, just as he didn't recognize the hundreds of other faces he saw every day of people who surely knew who *he* was, people who had even convinced themselves that they knew what was hidden in his heart, God love them. And heaven knows this man was right, Elvis didn't owe him a single thing.

Suddenly, there was a tap at the open office door. Elvis looked up. Silhouetted against the corridor lights were Gene Nelson and the Colonel.

"Busy?" Gene asked.

"Kind of," Elvis said.

"Just wanted to tell you I checked the dailies and there's a little problem—we keep seeing Wayne's face in the hoedown.

Can't cut around it, so we'll have to reshoot tomorrow morning. Only a half day, okay?"

Elvis clasped a hand to his forehead. At this particular moment, the prospect of prancing around hay bales for even one more minute felt like a twenty-year sentence on a chain gang.

"I told Gene we don't having anything else scheduled for tomorrow," Colonel Parker said brightly, sauntering toward his desk.

Reflexively, Elvis spread his hands over Littlejon's letter, but it was too late—Parker's eagle eyes saw it, and he was already shooting Elvis one of his scolding stares, the kind that said, *"Don't get distracted by that nonsense, son. Keep your eyes on the prize!"*

"No problem at all, Gene. I'll be there bright and early," Elvis said evenly, averting his eyes from Parker's. "But if you gentlemen will excuse me now, I got some personal business needs taking care of."

Colonel Parker fired off another admonishing glare but Elvis glared right back at him, and this time it was Parker who looked away. He must have seen the venom in Elvis's eyes, a look that said, *"Don't push me, Colonel, or I'll throw this damned desk lamp right in your face!"*

The moment the two men left, Elvis lifted the phone on Parker's desk and asked the MGM switchboard operator to connect him with the California Correction Institution in Tehachapi.

"I'd be happy to, Mr. Presley," the operator said. "Is there anyone in particular you wish to speak to?"

"Yes, ma'am," Elvis replied. "Man named Freddy Littlejon. He's doing time out there."

Elvis snapped off the lamp and put his feet up on the desk. Priscilla and the gang would be waiting for him at home. There had been talk of a wrap party out at the house to celebrate the completion of *Kissin' Cousins*. Of course, Priscilla would have heard about the Ann-Margret interview by now. He definitely wasn't looking forward to the conversation they would be having about that. It was hard enough having two opposite feelings about everything without a woman with tears in her eyes begging you to have one pure heart.

The operator said, "Go ahead," and a man's voice said, "Mr. Presley?"

"Yes, this is Elvis."

"My Lord, what a fine surprise this is," the man on the phone said. "I'm Bob Reardon, warden of CCI. Funny thing is, I just this minute heard them talking on the radio about you. About an interview you gave this afternoon."

"How about that?" Elvis said. Trifling news traveled fast out here in California.

"I hear you want to talk to one of our residents," the warden said. "Squirm Littlejon."

"That's right, sir," Elvis said.

"Call me Bob, please," the warden said.

"Okay, Bob."

"Did you want to meet with Squirm in person?"

"Just on the phone should do it," Elvis said.

"Between you and me, Mr. Presley, you can't tell much from a phone call with a con. Gotta see their eyes, you know?"

Elvis rubbed his jaw. What was this Reardon fella getting at?

"Normally, setting up a face-to-face is no easy thing," Warden Reardon went on. "Takes a load of paperwork. But I've been known to make exceptions under special circumstances."

"That's encouraging to hear," Elvis said.

"What are you doing right now, Mr. Presley?" the warden blurted out abruptly, with a self-conscious laugh.

Elvis gazed out the picture window of the Colonel's office. It was completely dark on the lot now, probably past eight o'clock already. What was Mr. Presley doing right now? He was sitting alone in a dark room in a movie studio trying like crazy to put off going home.

"Not a whole lot," Elvis answered.

"Well, if you got yourself in a car this minute, you could be up here by ten. And I'd have Mr. Squirm Littlejon waiting for you in a clean shirt and pants."

Elvis hesitated only a moment. "I'll be there," he said.

Reardon gave him directions, then signed off with, "I've got a little surprise for you myself, Mr. Presley."

3
SQUIRM

A LARGER-than-life portrait of President Kennedy hung on the wall behind Warden Reardon's desk looking like one of those oversized pictures of Jesus with doleful eyes that followed you everywhere you went. Reardon, a red-haired man with a boxer's compact body, bounced out of his chair the moment Elvis entered and pumped his visitor's hand energetically.

"Have any trouble finding your way?" the warden asked.

"No, sir. . . . No, Bob," Elvis replied. "Went just fine." In fact, the two-hour drive up Route 14 past Santa Clarita and Lancaster and into the mountains had put Elvis in a meditative mood. By the time he'd reached Tehachapi, he'd promised himself to take more long drives alone like this one—it helped a man reconnect with himself.

"I've got Squirm waiting in the conference room," Reardon said. "Is he a friend of yours?"

"We were in the army together," Elvis said.

"Hot damn! That's what he's always saying. Says he spent Christmas with you over there in Germany."

"That's right."

"How about that?" Reardon said. "I guess the little man was telling the truth for once."

"That something he's not in the habit of doing?"

"Truth is a real scarcity up here at CCI, Mr. Presley," Reardon said. "There's not a man in here that doesn't tell at least one big whopper a day, and it's usually the same damned one." Grinning, the warden gave Elvis a mock punch in the biceps before going into a burlesque whine, "'I didn't do it! I swear, I didn't! I was home in bed the whole time!'"

Reardon let loose a surprisingly high-pitched laugh, watching Elvis's face expectantly, apparently looking for appreciation of his little performance. Like most everybody Elvis met in California, the man was auditioning.

"I see what you mean," Elvis said.

Reardon pushed a buzzer on his desk and two muscular guards entered, one white and one black. Then, walking in what was apparently standard formation—one guard ahead of them and one behind, Elvis and Reardon made their way down a long corridor, passing through three barred gates, until they arrived at the conference room. Reardon grasped Elvis's sleeve.

"Take as long as you want with him, Mr. Presley," he said. "But when you're finished, don't forget I've got that surprise I promised you." He signaled one of the guards to open the conference-room door.

Freddy Littlejon started to rise as Elvis entered, but immediately lost his footing and stumbled back into his metal chair, the leg irons on his ankles clanging against the chair legs.

"I can't believe this," Littlejon said. "My prayers have been answered."

"Good to see you," Elvis said, then added for Reardon's benefit, "Again."

Reardon left, leaving the two guards outside the door, but there were two more already inside the room, one behind Littlejon, the other behind the chair reserved for Elvis on the other side of a Formica-topped table. Both guards went bug eyed when they saw Elvis, but neither said a word.

Squirm Littlejon was even slighter and more boyish looking than Elvis had surmised from the photograph. The thick, iron manacles on his wrists—joined together by no more than six links of chain—dwarfed his narrow wrists and spindly hands, making him look like little Hansel in the witch's cage. The loopy grin and sleepy eyes were the same as in the photo though; he had the half-frightened, half-insolent smirk of the boy who the teacher always caught dozing in class. Heaven knows, he didn't look like a murderer but, then again, neither had that kid who'd murdered all those fan-club presidents in Tennessee three years back.

Elvis sat down. "Start at the beginning," he said softly.

Littlejon cocked his head one way, then the other. "I been planning this for months, now here you are, and I can't figure where the beginning is. It's like every beginning has a beginning of its own."

"Just jump in anywhere," Elvis said. "Maybe at that Christmas party."

"Okay, I'll start right there in Germany, Christmas Day, 1959," Littlejon said. "You see, the 'home' I was missing while you were singing was just one person, my mother, Agnes. She'd brought me up by herself after my father took off. I was only two then and don't remember him, wouldn't know him if he was sitting next to me in a bar. Or in a cell, for that matter."

Littlejon offered Elvis a cheesy grin before going on.

"Anyway, I wasn't much for school. Pretty awful, actually. They said I had an attitude problem, and they were right about that. Around about the time they got to long division, I didn't see the point anymore. I mean, I just knew that long division wouldn't be figuring too much in any kind of life I'd be leading. Anyhow, I dropped out soon as I could, knocked around a bit, and then joined the army, telling them I was eighteen when I was barely past sixteen."

Elvis nodded encouragingly and Squirm went on.

"Well, overseas, I made friends with a guy named Macy—Phil Macy—and he told me I had a talent that could make me one heck of a good living when I got out. It was the way I could jump and twist and wiggle out of things, like the way I could slither through a drainpipe on bivouac."

Here Squirm gave a little pantomime demonstration, twisting his head and shimmying his shoulders like a snake slithering through a cotton field. It wasn't hard to figure where his nickname had come from. But there was also something about his little presentation that struck Elvis as familiar, although he couldn't remember where he'd seen it before.

"Macy said I could get a job doing the same thing he did back home," Littlejon continued. "Said I could be a stuntman in the movie pictures."

"So that's what you did?"

"That's right. I got into show business, just like you, Mr. Presley. Soon as I got out of the army, I made a beeline for Hollywood, looked up some people Macy told me about, and in one week's time I was working as a stuntman. Turns out I was a natural. It was like my mother always told me, everybody's got a God-given, special talent, but it's only the lucky ones who figure out what it is."

"My mother told me the exact same thing," Elvis said. He didn't add that, although he'd discovered his own God-given talent, lately he'd begun to wonder if he wasn't forsaking it.

"I could do it all," Littlejon went on. "Even if it was something I'd never done before. Like, first gig, I jumped off a galloping horse onto a runaway stagecoach like I'd been doing it my whole life. Same for leaping off cliffs and bursting through glass windows and running around in circles with my clothes on fire. And the thing is, because of my size and all, I was perfect for doing women's pranks. Made me feel kind of peculiar at first—dressing up in a ball gown to jump off a roof into a speeding convertible. But hell, I got twice the number of gigs as most of the other guys so I wasn't complaining. Fact is, I was king of the heap for a while there. Had myself a beautiful little house out by the beach. A brand new Oldsmobile. Even had myself a beautiful woman, an actress couple years older than me named Nanette Poulette, although that was just her made-up name. Nanette and me were going to get married."

For the first time since he started talking, Littlejon averted his eyes from Elvis's.

"What happened, Freddy?" Elvis asked softly.

Squirm squirmed around in his chair for a bit before getting himself to look back at Elvis.

"Okay, here goes," he said. "There was this little girl who played bit parts in pictures over at MGM. She'd have maybe one or two lines to speak, never anything more. Her name was Holly McDougal, and she'd pulled the same trick I had in the army, told everyone she was eighteen when she was really barely seventeen. Easy for her to pull off since she could have passed for twenty-one and then some if she wanted. She looked real grown-up, grown-up and sexy like a woman who'd been around the block a few times. And, the truth is, Holly may have been only seventeen, but she'd been around the block more times than most women twice her age."

Littlejon raised his manacled hands to his face in order to scratch his ear. This operation involved scraping the chain roughly across his chin—it must have been one devil of an itch to be worth it.

"You know that joke about the starlet who was so dumb she slept with the scriptwriter?" Squirm continued. "Well, Holly was so dumb she slept with the stuntmen. Every one of us. She was kind of a nympho, I guess. She'd come out to the stunt shack—you know, where we keep all our equipment and clothes and stuff—and take one of us off to this little curtained-off alcove in the back where we napped and, you know, she'd do us right there. Right there with everybody else smoking and joking and dressing up for a stunt only ten feet away."

Elvis lowered his eyes uncomfortably. For the first time since he'd impulsively phoned the California Correctional Institution a few hours back, he found himself wondering if he shouldn't have tossed that Christmas photograph back in the trash and left it at that. He honestly didn't know if he wanted to hear the rest of this indecent story.

"Understand, I'm not proud of this part, not at all," Squirm continued. "Actually, I'm real ashamed of it. Can't even say I didn't know what I was doing, although I really didn't know she was only seventeen. None of us did. But I did know there was something warped about the whole business. And I did know I had a perfectly wonderful woman waiting for me at home every night. I swear to God, if I had it all to do over again . . ."

"Keep going," Elvis prodded impatiently.

Littlejon shut his sleepy eyes for second, then opened them and went on.

"Well, on this particular day, I was the only one in the shack, so when Holly came by it was my turn. I went in the back with her and we made a quick business of it because I was due on the set in a few minutes. Anyhow, afterward, I left Holly back there and got dressed up to look like Paula Prentiss for a stunt in *The Honeymoon Machine*. The shoot went real late that night. The harness for my stunt kept getting stuck so it was almost midnight before we finished. And, when I got back to the shack, the police were there. Holly was dead, choked to death right in the cot where I'd left her. They arrested me right on the spot. And I've been behind bars one place or another ever since."

Elvis gazed intently into Littlejon's eyes. "And you didn't do it," he said.

"No, sir," Squirm replied.

"Who did, then?"

"I wish I knew," Squirm said. "I wish to God I knew."

"Who do you *think* did it?"

"I really don't know, Mr. Presley. Sometimes I think it might've been one of the other guys, the other stuntmen. I mean, when the trial came up every one of them swore on the Bible that they never even had sex with her. Of course, most of them were married, so that was probably the reason they did that."

Elvis drew in a deep breath and let it out slowly. "And what do you want me to do for you, Freddy?" he said wearily.

Squirm shrugged. "Get me out of here," he said softly.

"Just like that." Elvis smiled in spite of himself.

"Got to be some way," Squirm murmured. "I mean, it wouldn't be right to keep an innocent man locked up for the rest of his life, would it?"

For a long moment, Elvis just gazed across the Formica-topped table at Littlejon. The man seemed to be shrinking before his eyes. Another minute and he'd be able to just slip out of those manacles and leg irons and walk right out of here, slinking between bars and through keyholes and disappearing into the Tehachapi Mountains.

"I keep having this feeling I've seen you before," Elvis said finally. "Not just that Christmas Day."

"You have," Littlejon said quietly. "Just a little time after that. Out by your house on the Goethestrasse. It was a Sunday and one of the guys in my barrack brought me out for a football game. You and your friends from home against this pick-up team of GI's. We were both quarterbacks—me against you."

Now Elvis remembered that day precisely, remembered the skinny kid who could slither like a snake right through his line and make one touchdown after another until the middle of the game, when he just walked off the field without even saying a good-bye or a thank-you.

"Yes, I remember that day," Elvis said, smiling. "How come you left before the game was over?"

Squirm lowered his eyes.

"You get hurt?" Elvis asked.

"Not exactly," Squirm said. "I was kinda told to leave."

"Who told you that?"

"One of your friends," Squirm said softly. "Red, I think his name was. He told me I wasn't playing by the rules."

"Which rules?"

Littlejon looked up shyly. "The rule that says your team always has to win, Mr. Presley," he said.

From the corner of his eye, Elvis saw the guard behind Littlejon stifle a smirk. For a second, Elvis felt so angry he almost stood up right then and there and marched out. But the truth stopped him. And the truth was that he'd known full well about that rule, even if nobody ever said it out loud in front of him. He hated to lose and everybody knew that, so they made sure it never happened. Made sure that the King would never have to suffer the humiliation of defeat in a sandlot football game in a little town in Germany. But at this moment, Elvis was feeling a much worse humiliation—the humiliation of admitting to himself that he'd known about that rule and let it stand. That surely could not be healthy for a man's soul; it begged redemption.

"You must have a lawyer," Elvis said to Squirm Littlejon. "What's his name?"

"Had one," Littlejon said. "Man named Regis Clifford in West Hollywood."

"He still there?"

"Unless he's already drunk himself to death."

Elvis stood. "I'll be in touch, Squirm," he said.

Warden Reardon was waiting outside his office.

"The man on the radio said you were searching for the perfect movie script," he said to Elvis, grinning. "Said you didn't care who wrote it. And next thing I know, you're calling me up on the telephone. If that's not kismet, I don't know what is."

"Kismet?"

Reardon produced a large, maroon bellows envelope stretched to its limit.

"Well, you can stop searching now, Mr. Presley," he said, handing Elvis the envelope. "Here's your surprise—the script of a lifetime. True story. Nothing stranger than the truth, you know."

Elvis took it. "Thank you," he said.

Back in his car, Elvis took a quick look at the top page of the manuscript: *The Singing Prison Warden: My True Life Story* by Robert F. Reardon.

4
PERSONAL BUSINESS

PRISCILLA was waiting up for him. Two in the morning and she's sitting alone in their bedroom wearing that purple silk dress with the ruffled collar buttoned up to the neck, her black-dyed hair piled on top of her head like Mrs. John F. Kennedy's, except that she'd left a couple of ringlets hanging down on her forehead the way teenagers do. The rims of her sparkling dark eyes were pink from weeping, and there was a sorrowful pout on her sweet lips, but she held her head proudly erect and looked Elvis in the eye as he walked through the door. It was enough to break a man's heart.

He had phoned Ann-Margret over in England and she had told him she'd never said those things to the press, but Priscilla would never believe that. Only one way to handle a situation like this: Start at full throttle.

"Good thing that woman's over in London!" Elvis bellowed, striding toward Priscilla. "Otherwise she'd be missing a few teeth by now!"

Priscilla eyed him skeptically.

"Talking trash like that where I can't put a lid on her mouth!" Elvis rambled on, reaching out to wipe the tears from Priscilla's cheek.

Priscilla yanked back. "What *else* did you put on her mouth?" she snapped.

"That's no way to talk, darlin'."

Priscilla balled her little hand up in a fist, then shot a finger into Elvis's chest. "You've been with that woman, haven't you, Elvis?"

Elvis swallowed hard. "Not in the way you're thinking," he said.

"*What* way then?" Elvis had never seen her sweet young eyes look so hard.

"The *movie* way," he answered. He was improvising now. "Happens all the time when you're playacting lovers in a movie. Gets kind of confusing. You can't always stop dead in your tracks just because they put the cap back on the camera at the end of the day." There was some truth in that—just not the whole truth. Priscilla stared at him, tears welling in her eyes again.

"I . . . I'm going home," she whispered.

"Aw, darlin', don't say that."

"I am. I'm going back to Daddy where I belong."

"Please, darlin'." Elvis kneeled down in front of her at the side of the bed. "I couldn't even think of marrying a woman like Ann-Margret. Not when I got you waiting for me at home."

Priscilla's face still looked awful grim but the sniffling had stopped, so Elvis kept on talking at a fast clip, saying that what he needed from a woman was complete understanding and trust, and he knew he could never get that from an actress like Ann-Margret, who always put her career ahead of her personal life. Finally, he promised that he would never see Ann-Margret again, never even accept a movie role if she was going to be in the movie too.

"Honest and true?" Priscilla whimpered, raising her right hand in a kind of Scout's honor gesture.

"Honest and true," Elvis replied softly, although he did not raise his hand.

Priscilla settled down fast after that. They talked a while longer, deciding that the Colonel was probably right—it would be best if Priscilla went back to Memphis tomorrow and waited for him there so that the Hollywood gossip machine would get off both of their backs until this Ann-Margret thing blew over. And then there was nothing for either of them to do but to get undressed and into bed. It would have felt so right to make love to Priscilla after all of the emotion they had just been through together. To take that moment to finally break his rule of chastity with her. And God knows, Elvis had the feeling. He wanted to scoop her young body up in his arms and kiss it all over. But something stopped him and it wasn't just the usual reason—that he wanted her to be a virgin when they got married. No, what stopped him this time was the image of a naked teenage girl lying dead on a cot in MGM's stunt shack. It made his blood run cold and his sexual feelings go flat. He closed his eyes and nodded off to a dreamless sleep.

Joe knocked on the bedroom door at quarter to ten the next morning. Colonel was on the phone: Elvis was already an hour late for the reshoot. Elvis told Joe to tell the Colonel he was on his way, then made arrangements for Joe and his wife, Joanie, to take Priscilla to the airport for her flight back to Memphis. Joanie made him a stack of buttermilk pancakes and some sweet sausages, which he took out to the patio in the back.

It was another perfect sunny day on Perugia Way. The weather out here made Memphis seem positively frosty, yet there was something unsettling about it being the second week in November and not a yellow leaf in sight. It made it seem like time never passed, like he was trapped in a summer that would never end, and he missed the feeling that came with autumn, that feeling of gathering himself in like a caterpillar spinning itself into a cocoon, where he could sleep alone and dream of spring.

Trapped was the word, all right. Just about everything seemed like a trap these days—everything and everybody. Nibble the bait and the jaws snapped shut. *Gotcha, Elvis! Gotcha in my arms! Gotcha in my movie!* Elvis sawed off a chunk of sausage, dipped it in the melted butter, and stuck it in his mouth. But God knows, there was trapped and then there was *really* trapped. Now Freddy Littlejon, he was trapped for the rest of his life in a cell a quarter of the size of Elvis's swimming pool. And for doing something that he swore on his mother's grave he did not do. Of course, if he really was a murderer, swearing that he wasn't on his mother's grave probably would not present too much of a moral problem for him. You just couldn't tell.

Elvis reached for the phone on the glass-topped patio table and dialed information. "Regis Clifford in West Hollywood," he told the operator. "It's a business, ma'am, a law office."

There was only one Regis Clifford in West Hollywood, or in all of Greater Los Angeles for that matter. Elvis dialed the number and let it ring while he cut off a little wedge of pancake, mopped it around in sausage grease, and popped it in his mouth. The phone must have rung a good ten times before someone picked up, and then several seconds passed during which the receiver apparently dropped and bounced, then was picked up again, and a gravel voice said, "What?"

"I'm looking for Mr. Regis Clifford," Elvis said.

"What for?"

"Personal business," Elvis said.

"What kind?"

"I'd like to tell that to Mr. Clifford personally."

"Well, personally I *am* Mr. Clifford," the voice said. "Hold on a minute, would you?"

Elvis heard the unmistakable sound of liquid dribbling into a glass, then the strike of a match and a deep inhale.

"Had to get my breakfast," Clifford said.

"You sleep in your office?"

Clifford laughed. "That's right," he said. "It's one of the advantages of doing business with me—I'm on call night and day. . . . So what's on your mind, Mr.—?"

"Tatum," Elvis said, not really knowing why. "Jodie Tatum."

"So what can I do for you, Mr. Tatum?"

"I'm a friend of Freddy Littlejon's," Elvis said.

There was a stuttering cough at the other end. Finally, Clifford said, "Listen, Tatum, I did the best I could for that little weasel, no matter what he told you."

"I'm sure you did, Mr. Clifford," Elvis said. "I'm just wondering if there isn't something more we could do for him now."

"Like what? Get him room service?"

"Actually, I was wondering if there was a possibility of reopening his case," Elvis said, although this was the first time he had even put it to himself that way.

"And who would be footing for the bill for this particular enterprise?" Clifford asked.

"I would."

"Are you employed, Mr. Tatum?"

"Now and then," Elvis replied.

"How about now?" Clifford asked.

"What are your fees, Mr. Clifford?"

"A hundred dollars a day," Clifford blurted out.

"That shouldn't be a problem."

"Plus expenses," Clifford went on quickly. "That could bring it up to a good one-fifty to two hundred a day, depending on what's involved."

"I can manage that," Elvis said.

"Minimum of three days," Clifford said, his scratchy voice virtually rasping with excitement. "In advance, of course."

"Of course."

"I could clear my desk and get started on this immediately," Clifford said ecstatically.

"I'd appreciate that," Elvis said.

"Why don't you come right over?" Clifford said. "Unless, of course, you want me to come to wherever you are. I can do that. It'll cost you a little extra, of course."

"I'll come there," Elvis said.

Clifford gave him the address, telling him it was one flight up, over a record shop.

"I'll be right over," Elvis said.

"Mr. Tatum?"

"Yes?"

"Cash," Clifford said. "I like to do business in cash whenever possible."

"That can be arranged," Elvis said, and he hung up.

He finished off his breakfast, then brought his plate back into the kitchen where Joe and Joanie were stacking dishes in the dishwasher.

"The Colonel called on the other line," Joe said. "I told him you were just going out the door."

"Well, that is certainly true, Joey," Elvis said, smiling broadly. "I am just now going out the door."

5
COSMIC BALANCE

ELVIS drove to West Hollywood and parked his El Dorado convertible in a lot on West Third Street, then caught a cab to Clifford's place on West Eighth, all without being recognized, except by one person, the Mexican who managed the parking lot. He'd wanted Elvis to autograph a ticket stub and Elvis gladly obliged: "Miguel, Thanks for looking after my baby. Elvis."

In the taxi, he considered messing with his hair in an attempt at disguising himself for his meeting with Clifford. For a fleeting moment, he even wished that he'd worn that hateful blond wig— that might do it, although it hardly seemed likely. But what the heck, he was who he was, and the main thing was, his business with Clifford had absolutely nothing at all to do with who he was. Astounding how much comfort that thought gave him.

The record shop on the ground floor of Clifford's building was Mexican too, El Disco Norde, and its window was packed with 45s and albums in Spanish by people with Spanish names. But front and center was a 45 titled *The Lonely Bull* performed by a guy named Herb Alpert with a band called The Tijuana Brass. Next to it was an album entitled, *Rubias, Morenas Y Pelirrojas*, adorned with a picture of Elvis himself in a coat and tie. It was a kick seeing a photo of himself in the window of a store in a neighborhood he never even knew existed—and labeled in a foreign language at that. This was surely the part he liked the best about all that had happened to him in the last nine years—the way his music radiated out into the world and entered people's lives like a mystery man who walks in a stranger's front door and makes himself at home. But for the life of him, he didn't know what *Rubias, Morenas Y Pelirrojas* meant or even which of his albums it could be.

Elvis took the steps two at a time, then paused a moment to catch his breath on the second-floor landing. There were three doors with opaque glass windows, one for a travel agency, one for a chiropractor, and at the far end a partially opened door inscribed REGIS CLIFFORD. ESQ., ATTORNEY AT LAW, and under that in smaller letters, SPECIALIZING IN IMMIGRATION AND DIVORCE LAW. Elvis walked to it and peered inside.

It was a holy mess in there. It looked like a dingy, used bookstore that had suddenly changed its mind and become a single-occupancy room in a low-rent hotel—open books, unwashed plates, and an assortment of clothing crowding every available surface, including the window sills and a sink that was nestled below and between bookcases. Stooped over the sink with his back to him was a tall, slope-shouldered man in a loose-fitting black pinstriped suit with a cloud of smoke hovering over his head. He was washing dishes and singing to himself in a pretty decent baritone—some kind of folk song about flowers that bloom in the spring, *tra-la, tra-la*. Elvis knocked lightly on the door.

"Come in," the man said, still washing, not turning. "Be right with you."

Elvis stepped inside and waited until the man finished by wiping his hands on a gray-streaked towel. He turned and faced Elvis, a cigarette dangling from the corner of his mouth.

"Mr. Tatum?" he said.

For a split-second, Elvis felt confused. Or was it reflexive disappointment that the man actually did not recognize him?

"That's right," Elvis said. "Mr. Clifford?"

The man nodded, proffered his hand, but then quickly withdrew it. "Afraid my hands are still wet," he said. "I've been cleaning up. Big party here last night. Celebration. We won a major case."

"Congratulations," Elvis said, although he was pretty sure that it had been a party of one with nothing more to celebrate than the completion of the paperwork for a Tijuana divorce.

"I've got my Fredrick Littlejon file right over here," Clifford said, gesturing to a mahogany desk by the window. The desk, like Clifford himself, looked as if it had once been quite elegant, a patrician family heirloom that over time had suffered the indignities of ground-out cigarettes, spilt TV dinners, and the occasional swift kick of frustration. Three books lay open on top of it: one titled *Plutarch's Lives*, another called *The Psychopathology of Everyday Life*, by Sigmund Freud, and a fat one entitled *The Decline and Fall of the Roman Empire*. There was something fitting about that last one being here.

Elvis dug into his pocket and pulled out a roll of bills. He peeled off six hundred dollars in fifties and handed them to Clifford, saying, "Three days in advance with full expenses."

"I appreciate that, Mr. Tatum," Clifford said.

"Just call me, Jodie," Elvis said inexplicably, and feeling inexplicably amused for saying it.

"All right, Jodie," Clifford said, sitting behind his desk. "Let me give you my entire history with this case."

Elvis sat down across from him and listened. Littlejon had phoned Clifford from the L.A. county jail the day after his arrest, having gotten his name and number from a fellow stuntman named Mickey Grieves. Clifford had no idea who Grieves was at that point or why he'd recommended him, but one thing he did know was that once Grieves took the witness stand at the trial, he acted as if it was a foregone conclusion that Littlejon was guilty of the murder. He had even offered the court his theory of why Littlejon did it: because, in fact, Squirm had raped poor Holly McDougal, and when she threatened to go to the police, he killed her to shut her up.

"Is there any chance that's true?" Elvis asked.

"That's not for me to say, Mr. Tatum," Clifford replied coolly. "As Mr. Littlejon's attorney, I am not permitted to even entertain thoughts of his guilt."

Clifford delivered this line in clipped tones with an edge of haughtiness. Evidently, the six hundred dollars that had recently taken up residence in the pocket of his frayed pinstripe suit were prompting delusions of grandeur.

"Look, Mr. Clifford," Elvis said brusquely. "Littlejon's in jail doing life and I'm your client now. So I'd appreciate it if you'd just answer my question."

Clifford massaged his forehead a moment, as if trying to assuage a sudden migraine. "Yes, yes, of course, Mr. Tatum . . . Uh, what was the question again?"

"Is it possible that Littlejon did rape and kill the girl?" Elvis said.

"Yes, it's possible," Clifford replied. "Just about anything is possible in this case. You see, there weren't any witnesses, at least that we know of. Other than the perpetrator and the victim herself, of course. That Miss McDougal had recently engaged in sexual intercourse was never a question. Littlejon never denied that he'd, uh, had his way with her that day. There were bruises on Miss McDougal's body, especially around her neck, of course. She'd been choked to death with rubber tubing, something from one of the stunt apparatuses. So rape and murder certainly cannot be ruled out."

Elvis nodded. "Go on," he said.

Clifford said that he had taken Littlejon's statement right in his cell at the county lock-up. His story was basically the same as what he'd told Elvis last night: He and McDougal had had sex on the cot with no one around; he'd left her to go to work on a stunt for *The Honeymoon Machine*; when he returned to the stunt shack six hours later, the girl was dead and he was handcuffed and arrested immediately.

"Littlejon was convicted on circumstantial evidence, all of it, but there certainly was a mountain of it," Clifford said. "His fingerprints were all over the place—on Holly's belt buckle, her shoes, they even lifted one off her thumbnail. His day clothes were on the floor next to the cot. Someone had seen McDougal enter the shack late that afternoon when only Littlejon was in there. The fact is, Mr. Tatum, the only defense open to me was Littlejon's contention that this young woman was sleeping with virtually every stuntman in MGM's employ. Proving that would have at least taken some of the air out of the rape theory. But I couldn't prove that without witnesses, and I put one man after another on the stand—every stuntman who Littlejon said had slept with her—and one after another they denied it."

"Do you think someone set it up to look like Littlejon did it?" Elvis asked.

"That's a possibility," Clifford said. "Or it could have been a cover story that just happened to land in the murderer's lap after the fact. My guess is that it was a rage killing, not premeditated. Most killers don't plan a murder like that one—strangling a naked young woman in a bed. That says passion, not plan. So I don't imagine whoever did it was thinking about his alibi at the time. In fact, I don't imagine he was thinking at all. And that would include Littlejon himself if he was the murderer."

Suddenly, Clifford began vigorously rubbing his temples, apparently whacked by his migraine again. The lawyer's eyes darted around the room, then he jumped out of his chair and scooted behind Elvis to a bookcase where he immediately began rooting around. He was clearly not searching for a citation in a law text.

Elvis waited. He'd once had a drummer with this affliction, a curly-headed kid who drank a bottle of bourbon every day before noon to chase away his hangover from the night before. They had finally let him go after one performance when he slid off his stool and crashed into his standing cymbals in the middle of a ballad. It wasn't too hard to picture Regis Clifford sliding off his chair in the middle of a cross-examination.

Hanging on the wall behind Clifford's desk were several diplomas in cheap plastic frames. One was from a community college called Baywater. Elvis didn't know much about colleges, especially on the West Coast, but somehow that name did not sound promising. Another was a doctorate of law from a place called McGeorge Law School, and another was Clifford's certification that he had passed the California Law Boards in 1953. There were two more, both in Spanish. Above these, partly obscured by a calendar, was a small photograph in a gilt frame. Elvis squinted. A tall, white-haired man in judge's robes stood next to a fine-featured, smart-looking woman in a ball gown with a big hunk of jewelry around her neck. Standing in front of them were two boys, both in coats and ties and knickers, their hair slickly parted, looking like posh English schoolboys. Elvis stood and leaned over the desk to get a closer look. The boys were the same height and the same stringy build and their little jackets and ties were the same too. Fact was, except for the parts in their hair—one on the left, the other on the right—the two boys looked identical. *Twins.*

Elvis felt that familiar twist in his gut he experienced whenever he spotted twins. His own twin, Jesse Garon, had died the day they were born, yet there was not a day that went by that he didn't find himself thinking about him. Thoughts like, *Where would Jesse be now if he had lived? And what would he be doing?* Sometimes Elvis imagined the two of them singing together like the Everly Brothers, traveling from gig to gig in an open convertible, harmonizing country songs, joking with each other, reading each other's thoughts.

Clifford returned to his seat, wiping his mouth with the sleeve of his suit. "So, where were we?" he said earnestly, as if he had been interrupted by an important phone call.

"That you up there?" Elvis said, pointing at the photograph.

"One of them is," Clifford said.

"Identical, right?" Elvis said.

Clifford sighed, then offered Elvis an indulgent smile. "It's like the man said—one of us is identical, but the other one doesn't look like anybody." Clifford shuffled some papers on his desk. "We were talking about Littlejon's defense," he went on quickly, "at least, what little of it there was, considering what we had to go on."

Elvis would have liked to talk more about Clifford's twin, but it was clear that Clifford did not. No matter, that's not what he was here for.

"What did you find out about Holly McDougal from other folks?" Elvis asked. "Other actresses, her family, neighbors and the like."

"Not much," Clifford said. "All she had for family was a mother and a sister. The mother hung up on me whenever I phoned. Finally, I went out to their place, an apartment in a run-down neighborhood in East L.A., and got pretty much the same treatment there. She screamed at me through a crack in the door, saying she would not have me sullying the good name of her poor, dead, God-fearing daughter. She must have heard that I was trying to establish that her daughter had a weakness for stuntmen. Anyhow, I took the same kind of abuse from the neighbors. And I've told you about the other stuntmen. They'd go on and on about what a sweet kid Holly had been, so adorable and sincere, the kind of kid you'd want for a daughter."

"How about other people at MGM?" Elvis asked.

"I didn't get much from them either," Clifford said. "Not a very forthcoming bunch, considering the way those people will talk ad nauseam about just about anything once they get on the *Jack Parr Show*. Half the movies they do over there have somebody getting shot in the head or stabbed in the guts, but God forbid anybody should actually talk about a *real* murder. Not the polite thing to do. Which roughly translated means it would be bad publicity.

"But there was one exception, a makeup artist named Connie Spinelli. I got her on the phone at her home and she said that Holly McDougal was the wildest kid she ever knew. That she did all kinds of crazy things and told Connie all about them. She said that she had stories about Holly that would make a stripper blush to her ankles." Clifford's sallow face momentarily brightened. "Those were her exact words—'make a stripper blush to her ankles.' Droll image, eh, Jodie?"

"What exactly did she tell you about Holly?" Elvis asked.

"Not a thing, as it turned out," Clifford said. "We made a date to meet the next morning at a coffee shop near the studio. I waited two hours for her, then went over to MGM and asked if she'd come in yet. She hadn't. In fact, they said Miss Spinelli's employment with them had been terminated the day before. I called her at her home again, but there was no answer. And when I went out there later that day, a neighbor said that she had gone out the night before and not come back. She didn't come back the next day either. Or the next. And the day after that, we went to trial without the benefit of Miss Connie Spinelli's testimony."

"Have you tried to find her since then?" Elvis asked.

"It was a little late for that, don't you think?" Clifford shrugged defensively. "Look, Jodie, I don't know what your relationship with Mr. Littlejon is. And God knows, I appreciate the way you do business." Here, he patted his money-bulging pocket. "But I'd be misleading you if I told you we had a prayer of reopening this case, let alone of exonerating Littlejon."

"How come?"

"Because you haven't heard the worst of it," Clifford said. "Like about Miss Nanette Poulette, Littlejon's so-called girlfriend. If there were ever any doubts in the jury's mind before she took the stand, they were gone afterward. That woman handed them the keys to the California Correctional Institution and told them to lock Littlejon up and throw them away."

"What did she say?" Elvis asked.

"She said in no uncertain terms that her boyfriend was a sexual pervert. She said he liked to play sick little games at home with her. Dress-up games. He'd bring home costumes from the wardrobe room for her to wear, Little Bo Peep outfits and little schoolgirl outfits. Those were his favorites, she said, the schoolgirl outfits with short short kilts and pleated white blouses. She'd put them on and then he would chase her around the house, calling, 'Oh, little girl? Where are you? I'm going to get you, little girl.' And then when he caught her, he'd get rough with her. A good spanking for openers."

Elvis put his hand to his forehead. If there was one thing about human nature that he would never understand, it was why people were always trying to turn sex into something that it wasn't. They took this God-given beautiful thing and turned it into scum. It was a psychological problem, he'd read, but that didn't keep Elvis from feeling utter disgust when he heard stories like this one. And he didn't think he could stomach many more like it. Maybe it was time to bail out of this whole business. Call the six hundred dollars in Clifford's pocket an act of charity and get back to his real life.

"Littlejon denied the whole thing," Clifford abruptly went on. "He told me she made the whole thing up, and the truth is, I tended to believe him. Because Nanette's little courtroom performance seemed to break his heart more that anything else that happened to him. He said that he'd never had a more tender love in his whole life than the one he had for her. Of course, Littlejon blamed himself for Nanette's lie. He said she was probably so hurt to find out that he'd been playing around with Holly that she wanted to get back at him. Sometimes, he even said that he deserved to spend the rest of his life in prison just for that, just for cheating on the love of his life."

Once again, Elvis found himself feeling for that poor soul, Squirm Littlejon. "I don't suppose he has seen her since then," he said. "No visits."

"Not likely," Clifford replied. "From what I hear, she's been doing very well in the movie business. She changed her name back to Nancy Pollard and went into some kind of production work."

"Where?"

"MGM."

Elvis impulsively reached for the phone on Clifford's desk. "Mind if I make a call?"

"Depends on where to."

"Take it out of your expenses," Elvis snapped, dialing the studio and telling the switchboard operator that he wanted to speak with Tom Parker.

"Who should I say is calling?" the operator asked.

Elvis eyed Clifford. "Jodie," he said to the operator, "Jodie Tatum."

Parker picked up himself. "Where the hell are you?" was his greeting.

"Sorry I'm late," Elvis said. "Something came up."

"Damn it, Elvis, do you know what it costs to keep twenty-five people standing around on a movie set? And all of them union, right down to the second gaffer?"

"I'll cover it. Be there in an hour." Elvis hung up and nodded to Clifford. "Listen, I've got to be somewhere, Mr. Clifford. I'll see if I can find that stuntman, Grieves. Miss Pollard too. And if anybody knows what became of the Spinelli woman. Meantime, why don't you go out to Miss McDougal's neighborhood again and root around. I'd skip her mother and neighbors this time, but maybe you can find where she went to school and her church and people she knew there."

Clifford's eyes belied a flicker of anxiety. It probably wasn't simply the prospect of roaming around East L.A. that worried him—it was the prospect of having to leave his office at all.

"One last thing," Elvis said, standing and gesturing to Clifford's desk. "I'd like to take the transcript of Littlejon's trial with me. Bedtime reading."

Now Clifford looked seriously alarmed. "I, uh, I don't think that would be such a good idea," he stammered.

"Why not?"

"You see, there's only one copy, Mr. Tatum, and—"

"I'll take good care of it."

"It will just seem like a lot of mumbo-jumbo to you," Clifford persisted.

"You get a lot of experience with mumbo-jumbo in my business," Elvis replied, extending his hand across the desk. "Let's not waste time, Mr. Clifford."

Clifford reluctantly gathered up several sheaves of paper, stuck them helter-skelter into a file folder, and handed them to Elvis. He followed Elvis to the office door.

"Some people say that *everybody* has a twin," Clifford blurted out as Elvis was about to leave.

"What do they mean by that?"

Clifford shrugged, smiling grimly. "That whatever you do, there's somebody out there—your twin—doing the exact opposite thing at the same time."

"What the devil for?"

"Balance," Clifford said. "Cosmic balance."

6
O SHINE ON ME!

ELVIS came trotting into Colonel Parker's office at one-fifteen, one hour to the minute after he'd phoned.

"Do me a favor, Colonel," he said, unbuttoning his shirt. "Call down to makeup and say I'm on my way. Likewise to wardrobe. I'll be on the set in thirty minutes flat. You tell Gene I'm just aching to dance the hoedown."

Colonel glanced up at him from his desk, a disdainful expression on his face. "You seem awful cheerful for a man who just skimmed four thousand dollars off our profits," he said.

"Got to be," Elvis replied, slipping out of his shirt and tossing it on a chair. "There's a lot of sorrowful people out there. Got to keep the balance."

"Well, while you're feeling so chipper, you might want to take a look at this morning's mail." Parker wagged his head toward the corner. Two more peach crates had been added, both of them brimming with film scripts. "Sixty-five so far, and that's before the morning papers came out," Parker said. "But you'll be pleased to hear that at least three of them are by truck drivers. Didn't see any by fishermen though."

"Actually, it's sixty-six," Elvis said blithely, already on his way out the door. "I got one hand delivered to me last night."

Madge Dickerson greeted him at the makeup department door with, "So, who are you today, Elvis?"

"Jodie," Elvis replied, settling into the leather-padded chair. "Well, then it's a good thing I snatched that wig back from Mr. Parker," she laughed. "That man was growing attached to it."

"He always wanted to be a blond," Elvis said, closing his eyes tight as Madge began lathering on the tawny foundation that was supposed to give Jodie Tatum a woodsy appearance to contrast with the soft, pale face of his look-alike cousin, Lieutenant Josh Morgan. "You've been here quite some time, haven't you, Miss Madge?"

"Too long," Madge intoned. Elvis could picture the expression of mock despair on Madge's face as she said this. She was a hefty woman in her late forties who dyed her hair a different color every week "just to keep the mirror from getting bored" she explained. Madge encouraged the impression that she'd seen it all in her day and was not about to get excited by finding any celebrity perched in her makeup chair, not even Elvis Presley.

"Then I suppose you remember a gal named Connie Spinelli who used to work down here," Elvis said, trying to keep it casual.

"Yup," Madge replied, not missing a beat as she patted Elvis's face with a cotton ball to soak up the excess foundation.

"Whatever happened to her, you know?" Elvis went on as if he was just passing the time of day.

"Couldn't say," Madge said. Then, "Going to do your lashes now, honey, so don't squeeze so tight, okay?"

Elvis did as he was told. "Couldn't say or wouldn't say?" he said.

"Just *not* saying," Madge said, giving the ends of Elvis's lashes a smart upturn. She'd once told Elvis that he had the longest lashes of any man she'd worked on since Clark Gable.

"I'd sure like to talk with her, Madge," Elvis continued.

"Connie was a talker, all right," Madge said. "And that's a terrible quality for people in our line of work. We hear it all down here, you know. Something about sitting in this chair and being fussed over makes people open up like they were in confession. And that's why we learn to keep our own mouths shut. Most of us, that is." She fitted a net over Elvis's head and tied it tight. "It's wig time, sailor," she said.

Elvis opened his eyes to see himself in duplicate in Madge's hinged mirror—that blond hillbilly, Jodie Tatum, again. So which twin was he? The one out in the world doing the right thing? Or the other one balancing the good deeds with iniquity.

He rose from the chair, clutching the makeup towel around his neck. There didn't seem any sense in pressing Madge any further about Connie Spinelli. Truth was, Elvis felt a grudging respect for her after all the blabbermouths who had served him a hamburger or filled his gas tank and then gone running to the nearest phone to call the newspapers and repeat every little word he had said to them.

"Thank you, Miss Madge," he said, going out the door. He paced down the hallway toward the wardrobe room.

"Mr. Presley?"

Elvis turned his head. For a fraction of a second, he couldn't see who it was who had called his name. But then he spied a tiny Chinese woman huddled between the water cooler and the wall. She looked frightened.

"Ma'am?"

"I know Connie," the woman whispered. "I hear you ask."

Elvis walked up close to her. Now he remembered where he'd seen her before; she was in charge of clean-up detail in the makeup room.

"Do you know where she is?" Elvis asked.

"Atlanta. Atlanta, Georgia," the woman replied, still whispering. "She work in beauty salon there. Don't know name."

"How do you know she's there?"

"She send my boy a birthday card," the woman said. "She love children. Very good person, Connie."

They both heard footsteps coming up behind them—it was a young man lugging an open box full of cowboy hats. He had that cocky air of most of the go-fers who worked on the lot, a look that said it was merely a matter of months before he'd be running the studio.

"Always happy to sign an autograph, ma'am," Elvis intoned loudly for the go-fer's benefit, patting the Chinese woman on the shoulder. He waited until the young man had passed, then thanked the woman for her help.

She looked up at Elvis beseechingly. "Please, Mr. Presley," she said. "Do not say I tell you. I need job very much."

"Cross my heart," Elvis said. "And God bless you, ma'am."

Five minutes later, Elvis walked on to Sound Stage G in full Jodie Tatum regalia. "Beg your pardon, folks," he called out to the actors and crew who'd been waiting for him since morning. "Something came up."

A chorus of "That's okay, Elvis" and "No problem" came back at him. They were an obliging bunch, even if a sizeable part of their goodwill came from the fact that they were being paid in full for loitering on the set half the day. The assistant director saluted Elvis and called for everyone to hit their marks for the first take. They were just going to do four pickups from the hoedown sequence for coverage, he said, then he signaled a technician to start running the playback so they could get the rhythm in their bones. And there it was again, that god-awful singsongy riff on a Virginia reel, but this time it didn't grate on Elvis the way it had every time before; it was simply background noise for a job to get done and over with as quickly as possible.

Wayne LeFevre was in army uniform playing Josh Morgan today. As he sauntered past Elvis to take up his position, he gave Elvis a sardonic grin and said, "Been playing hooky again, pal?" Then Gene Nelson stepped out from behind the camera and gave his pithy directorial instructions: "Listen up, people. Look happy as pigs in clover, okay?"

They rewound the tape with the speakers still on; played backward, the piece had an eerie, Oriental sound—an improvement, Elvis thought, but nonetheless he readied himself to dance with a smile and a twinkle to rival any hog's. Gene called, "Action!" and off they went. Elvis jumped to it like a teenager at a state fair, swinging and spinning and leaping over hay bales with his head tossed back and his hips swiveling. It felt good to throw himself into it completely. Funny how not giving a hoot about the whole thing freed him up. They were done, close-ups and all, in less than an hour and half.

As Elvis was leaving, LeFevre fell in alongside of him. "I'm going to miss this, partner," he said, winking. "I just love being you, man." Elvis gave him a bemused smile. On location up in Big Bear, LeFevre had made a pass at every female he came within ten feet of, regardless of whether she was attached or remotely interested in him—even pretty much regardless of how she looked. He'd beam that hundred-watt grin of his, tell the girl in question that she was the most delectable little thing he ever did see, and then, often as not, suggest that he was already seriously considering marrying her. If he struck out—which seemed to happen nine times out of ten—he'd just bow and grin and say that it was surely a terrible waste of a divine opportunity, then turn to the next one and start all over again. More than once, immediately after Elvis had politely spurned the advances of some chorus girl on the set, LeFevre had appeared in a flash, telling the girl how badly he felt for her, but to cheer up because he, himself, was her consolation prize. "Hey, I'm almost Elvis anyhow," he'd tell her. "Except *I* got all the time in the world for you." When it came to chasing women, one thing old Wayne had going for him was an utter lack of pride.

"See you again sometime, Wayne," Elvis said.

"Hope so," Wayne replied. He angled his large head—the exact same size as Elvis's—to Elvis's ear. "But not soon, I figure. You're going back East tomorrow, right?"

Elvis shot him a quizzical look. "Oh, I'll be around for a bit," he said.

Wayne appeared distressed for a second, but then quickly resumed his boyish grin. "Well, you just keep sending the overflow in my direction, okay, pal?"

Back in his dressing room, Elvis closed the door and slid the bolt shut. He picked up the phone and gave the switchboard operator a number in Alamo, Tennessee. A minute later, he heard a young woman's soft Southern voice say, "William Jackson Clinic. How may I help you?"

Elvis couldn't speak. It was not Selma's voice. Of course, it wasn't. But at that moment, those words and that soft voice warmed his blood and cradled his heart as if it really were Selma DuPres on the other end of the line, as if the one woman he had ever loved fully and unconditionally were still alive and working in his good friend Billy Jackson's medical clinic in the black section of Alamo. Elvis tried his best not to think about Selma any more. But truth to tell, he thought about her every day.

"I'd like to speak with Doctor Jackson, please," Elvis said at last. "If he's not too busy, that is."

"Who's calling?"

"Just a friend," Elvis said. "An old friend."

"It's Mr. Presley, isn't it?" the woman said. Elvis could hear the easy smile in her voice and it made his heart ache even more.

"Yes, Ma'am, it is," he said.

"I'll get him for you," the woman said.

While he waited, Elvis heard the familiar sounds of Billy's waiting room in the background—the crying babies, the laughing mothers, even the rolling snores of the elderly folks who lined the chairs along the wall, folks who came in every day just because it made them feel safe and comfortable to be there. Probably even more of them were showing up since the air conditioning had been put in—Elvis's gift to the clinic last Christmas.

"Well, as I live and breathe," Billy said as he came on the phone. "How are you doing, Mr. P.?"

"Okay, Billy. How about yourself?" Elvis said. God, it was good to hear Billy's voice again.

"Middling to fair," Billy said with a laugh. "We've got ourselves a new strain of flu down here. Virus must come from all those Northern kids buzzing around town registering us colored folks to vote."

"The bad with the good, huh?"

"Bad's worth the good in this case," Billy said.

"Amen to that," Elvis said. Then, "I see you've got a new nurse working for you."

"That I do, Elvis," Billy said softly, a tenderness in his voice. The man knew instinctively how hearing the new girl's voice must have affected Elvis. "I put flowers out in the cemetery every week like you asked," Billy went on. "And I speak your love to Selma."

"I truly appreciate that, Billy," Elvis said, his eyes spontaneously filling up.

"So what can I do for you, Mr. P.?" Billy asked, sounding sunny again.

Elvis swallowed hard. "I want to ask a favor," he said.

"Shoot."

"I need to locate a woman named Connie Spinelli," Elvis said. "She's in Atlanta working in a beauty parlor. That's all I know. But I'd like you to find her and tell her to call me immediately. Collect, of course. Or get her number and I'll call. Tell her it's important. Somebody's life depends on it."

"I see," Billy said.

"I know you're busy, Billy," Elvis went on. "So you just tell me if you can't do it and I'll understand."

"It sounds like something I could make the time for," Billy said.

"I appreciate that, Billy," Elvis said. "I'll wire you money for the fare and expenses."

"Could be one little problem though," Billy said. "Miss Spinelli is white, I imagine. And it's going to take more than a few hundred Northern kids to change the way they do business in Atlanta. I'm not sure how welcome a black man is going to be in a white woman's beauty salon. I'm willing to try, though."

"That's all any of us can do," Elvis said. "Try and try again."

"So tell me, Mr. P, does this mean you're back in the detective business again?" Billy laughed.

"Just playing at it," Elvis said, feeling a tinge of embarrassment. "You know, Billy, one time when I was feeling awful foolish about snooping around those fan-club murders, I told Selma that the worst thing about doing detective work was that it made me feel so good. So alive, you know. And Selma said to me that working for you made her feel good for the same reason. Because doing things for other people has a way of getting you outside yourself, and the more outside yourself you get, the more alive you feel inside. I've never forgotten that."

"She was one wise woman," Billy said. "God bless her."

"I miss her terrible, friend," Elvis said softly.

"I know that, Elvis. But tell me honestly, how are you doing otherwise?"

For some reason, tears welled up in Elvis's eyes again. He had to wait a couple of seconds before answering.

"I'll tell you, Billy, it's not just Selma's sweetness I miss," Elvis said quietly. "It's the sweetness in my own soul. Sometimes . . . sometimes I think it's all dried up on me."

"I know that feeling," Billy said, and then, "Say, you want to hear a song?"

"A song?"

"Yup, a new one to me. Heard it in church last Sunday."

"When did you start going to church, Billy?"

"I just go for the music," Billy said, laughing.

"Let's hear that song," Elvis said.

Billy cleared his throat. Then, in his spring-clear tenor he began to sing a gospel song:

> *"There's a dark place, Lord,*
> *A hidden place no light can reach,*

No sound can breach,
No preacher preach.

There's a dark place, Lord,
A hidden place so deep in my heart,
In the deepest part,
In the saddest part.

Shine on me!
O Shine on me!
O Shine on me!
O Shine on me!"

Elvis was crying full out now, the tears streaming down his face. "Thank you, brother," he said.

"You take care of yourself, Elvis," Billy said. And they hung up.

7
THE STUNTMAN'S MISTRESS

IT TOOK a good ten minutes for all the tears to flow out of him. Where did all that sorrow came from? Missing Selma? Missing his mother? His lost twin, Jesse? Or was it something else too, a hidden place in his soul desperately seeking light.

Finally, Elvis stood up, went to the sink and splashed his face with cold water. He took a deep breath and let it out, then took another and another. He looked at his watch: almost four o'clock. Priscilla would be high over the Midwest by now. There was no denying he was relieved that she was going back to Memphis. The film was now completely finished and he would join her soon. But not yet. No, not just yet.

Elvis dialed the MGM operator again. "I'm looking for a woman named Nancy Pollard," Elvis said. "What department would she be in?"

"Miss Pollard? Why, she's head of development, Mr. Presley."

"Would you connect me to her, ma'am?"

The extension rang just once before it was picked up and a bubbly voice said, "Development. Miss Aronson speaking."

"Hello, Miss Aronson. This is Elvis Presley and I'm looking for Miss Pollard."

"Why, *hello*, Mr. Presley," Aronson gushed. "Nancy, uh, Miss Pollard, was wondering if you would call. I must say, I didn't think you would."

"She was expecting to hear from me?" Elvis asked warily.

"She was indeed," Aronson bubbled on.

"Why would that be, ma'am?"

"Because of the search you're on, of course," Aronson said.

What the devil was going on here? He had only seen Littlejon last night and Clifford this morning—how could word already be out that he was looking into the case? Who had blabbed? Warden Reardon? One of the prison guards? Madge Dickerson, in spite of her riff on the makeup artists' honor code? Or maybe the MGM operator had been listening in on his calls—that would explain it. When it came to gossip, Los Angeles was about the size of Tupelo.

"What exactly do you know about my search?" Elvis asked tersely.

"Just what I read in the papers," Aronson said. "That you're looking for a story with some real substance. A script that can reach way down and inspire. A *quality* film."

It was all Elvis could do to keep from bursting out laughing. "That's right, Miss Aronson," he said. "That's why I want to talk with Miss Pollard."

"Well, I don't want to step on anybody's toes," Aronson said in an intimate whisper, "but personally I have some marvelous properties that would be just perfect for you. Serious things. James Dean kind of things."

"Glad to hear that," Elvis said. "But I'd like to meet with Miss Pollard. May I speak with her?"

"Oh, she's still out at lunch," Aronson said. Four o'clock and still at lunch—Nancy Pollard certainly had come up in the world since she was Nanette Poulette. "I could set something up for tomorrow though. Are you free for lunch?"

"I guess I am," Elvis said. "But I don't much like eating out in this town, if that's okay."

"I'll order in," Aronson said. "You like baby back ribs, if I'm not mistaken."

"When they're done right," Elvis said reluctantly. He didn't add that the few times he'd tried ribs in California restaurants they had tasted more like Swiss steak out of a pressure cooker than the real, smoked thing.

"One o'clock then. All right, Mr. Presley?"

"I'm looking forward to it," Elvis said.

He set down the phone and walked to the window. Out on the lot, an entire battalion of extras in World War I infantry uniforms was ambling by. Several had bloody-looking bandages bound around their heads; one was naked to the waist with a half-dozen simulated bullet holes in his chest; another was on wooden crutches with one pant leg pinned up to the knee. A one-legged man could probably make a decent career as an extra in Hollywood. Like Squirm said, Everybody's got a God-given, special talent, but it's only the lucky ones who figure out what it is.

Elvis took the stairs down to the first floor and was strolling on the lot before he realized that he was still wearing Jodie Tatum's hillbilly costume and blond wig. Not that it mattered. One good thing about life in this dream factory was that no one took any notice of you whatever you were wearing or not wearing, or whoever you were. It was an unwritten rule on the lot that nobody could approach you for an autograph or a handshake. Actually, the extras and chorus girls and boys seemed to like that rule: for at least a few minutes each day, it put them on equal footing with the stars.

Elvis figured it for the stunt shack the minute he saw the small building at the far end of the lot. It looked a lot like a moonshine hut back home—no windows, low on one side and high on the other where the still would be—and leaning against the side wall were all manner of weapons: muskets, machine guns, lances, Samurai swords. But the telltale clue was the mini trampoline in front. A rangy, unshaven man in a cowboy shirt, leather vest, dungarees and chaps was bouncing up and down on it in stocking feet, effecting a half turn while drawing two six-guns from hip holsters on every other upward vault. It was a marvel to behold. The man had the easy grace of a dancer, but the weathered face and muscular build of a Green Beret. Elvis watched until the stuntman finished up with an airborne somersault and landed on his feet, right in front of Elvis, his six-guns pointing straight at him.

"You've got yourself a real talent there," Elvis said.

"I've heard the same about you, Mr. Presley," the man replied with a sly grin. He holstered both guns and extended his hand. "Name's Cathcart. Will Cathcart."

"Pleasure to meet you, Will," Elvis said, shaking his hand.

"Pleasures all mine," Cathcart said. "You just poking around or is there something I can do you for?"

Up close, Cathcart looked no more than nineteen or twenty. He had only appeared older because his skin had taken a real beating from the sun, but underneath the leathery tan and the stubble was a lingering case of acne that neither could camouflage. He was not a good-looking boy, but it didn't much matter in his line of work—you were never supposed to see the stuntman's face.

"Just poking," Elvis replied. "I've never been out this way before. I always wondered where you guys hung out."

"Want me to show you around?"

"I'd be obliged."

Elvis had to stoop to follow the young stuntman through the door into the low end of the shack. Save for the daylight streaming in through the open door, it remained dark as a cellar in there until Cathcart snapped on the overhead lights. The place looked like a toy and sport store gone crazy, every inch of space covered with beach balls, harnesses, lariats, padded vests, padded overalls, Stetson hats, horse whips, snorkeling gear, a staircase that went up four steps then stopped in mid-air, boots with rappelling cleats, ropes, hooks, a couple of fire extinguishers, and clothes racks loaded down with everything from togas to astronaut suits to fancy ball gowns. There were at least a dozen other items that Elvis could not identify—a rubber bodysuit with feathers fastened to the front and back like some kind of giant sea bird, long-handled objects with loops or hooks or long steel blades at their ends, Rube Goldberg-like hook and pulley apparatuses. The tools of the stunt trade. Rubber tubing was an integral part of at least half of these items.

Directly to Elvis's right was an interior curtain that was drawn closed. "Storage?" he said, pointing to it.

"Bunk room," Cathcart replied. "Just a couple of cots."

"Mind if I take a gander?"

"Not much to see," the young man said, pulling back the curtain.

Elvis gazed inside. The scene of Holly McDougal's murder looked like nothing so much as a high school kid's slovenly bedroom—two unmade cots, clothing and shoes strewn all over the floor, girly calendars on the wall, and here and there plaques and chrome-plated cups that appeared to be varsity football awards but on closer inspection turned out to be rodeo trophies. From his experience with the fan club murders, Elvis knew that the scene of a horrendous crime usually turned out to be the most ordinary of places—a bedroom, a kitchen—but nonetheless he was struck by the sheer innocence of this little coop.

Elvis stepped into the room. According to Clifford, one of the pieces of circumstantial evidence that had convicted Littlejon was the fact that his street clothes were found on the floor next to McDougal's body. That surely had to be pretty slim evidence if the floor looked anything like this on a regular basis. On the other hand, the eyewitness who had declared that Littlejon and McDougal were alone in here that afternoon only needed to have a clear view of the front door to make his claim—it was the sole entrance and exit and there were no windows.

Elvis gazed at the young man's face. Cathcart had not seemed at all nervous about showing him the bunk room. "You been at this work for long?" Elvis asked.

"Not very," Cathcart said. "I'm rodeo, you know. But that doesn't put much food on the table, and I've got three and a half mouths to feed. Wife's got a little one cooking in the oven right now."

Elvis smiled. He had noticed that the boy had the bowed legs and curved spine of a veteran rodeo rider. "So you just do this part-time?"

"I do whatever comes up," Cathcart said. "But these days if I gotta choose between a rodeo gig and a stunt gig, I go for the stunt. Three times the money. And most folks don't believe it, but it's a whole lot safer jumping off a trampoline with your clothes on fire than being thrown by a bull who's got his balls in a slipknot."

"So when'd you start stunt work?" Elvis asked.

"Last year," the boy said. "Had to wait until I turned eighteen. Otherwise the insurance don't cover you."

That put Cathcart here well after the murder.

"Ever hear about a girl named Holly McDougal?" Elvis asked.

"Nope," the boy said. "She a singer?"

"Actress," Elvis said. "At least she was. She's dead."

"Sorry to hear that. She a friend of yours?"

"Kind of," Elvis said.

"Well, the good Lord takes 'em all, don't He? I lost my best buddy just this year. Kicked in the head by a crazy pony and never came to."

"I'm sorry," Elvis said.

Cathcart shrugged. "Over here's the fun house," he said, gesturing to the end of the shack where the ceiling abruptly shot up another ten or twelve feet. "Want to take a look-see?"

"Sure do," Elvis said.

This end of the shack was as clean and uncluttered as the other side was a pig sty. Not a thing on the floor except wall-to-wall gym mats which extended a couple of yards up the wall as well. The centerpiece was a nylon cable which hung down from a beam at the apex of the A-frame ceiling. Swaying from the bottom of the cable was a leather chest and shoulder harness, a formidable-looking cross-hatch of belts and buckles that laced up in the back like an old-fashioned corset.

"This here's Nelly, the stuntman's mistress," Cathcart laughed, giving the harness a push that sent it in a wide arc which grazed the wall. "Gotta treat her sweet or she'll drop you faster than a lead balloon."

Elvis grabbed the harness as it swung toward him. "Use it for jumping?"

"Mostly for climbing," Cathcart said. "Say you're scaling the side of a building or up a stony ledge. Like one of the old-timers was in a picture where this guy had to climb up George Washington's face on Mount Rushmore. They brought a crane up there, hung a cable from the end, and attached it to old Nelly strapped under his shirt. I seen the movie. You can spot the cable if you know where to look, even though they tried to fool you by painting it sky blue." He grinned at Elvis. "Want to take her for a spin?"

Elvis hesitated. Only a few weeks back he'd told the Colonel that he'd like to do some of his own stunts in his next picture. He thought it might help keep his interest up if he was going to do anymore sleepwalkers like *Kissin' Cousins*. Of course, the Colonel had said absolutely not. "Son, you've got a face like a Botticelli angel," Parker had said. "We can't be jeopardizing a thing like that."

"Sure, why not?" Elvis said to Will Cathcart.

Elvis removed his shirt and put on a T-shirt that Cathcart picked randomly off the floor on the other side of the shack. It was a bit snug, especially across his mid-section, but Elvis barely noticed after the kid buckled and laced him into the stuntman's mistress; the harness itself was so tight it chafed against his ribs with every inhale.

"I'm going to take you up a couple feet, okay, Mr. Presley?"

"What do I do?"

"Whatever you please, Elvis," the boy said. "You could act like you're climbing up George Washington's face if you wanted. Nellie will do all the real work."

The boy vanished from Elvis's sight. "Here goes!" he called.

Elvis was yanked up so fast his head snapped forward and his insides churned. The straps under his shoulders pinched his skin so viciously that his eyes smarted. But the worst part was the dizziness—the dizziness and the feeling of vulnerability. He felt like a puppet. And that was surely a feeling he did not like at all.

"Sure hope you know what you're doing, Will," Elvis said, forcing a little laugh.

"Oh, I know what I'm doing, all right," Cathcart chimed back. "I learned from the master."

"The master?"

Abruptly, Elvis was hoisted up another five feet. He was now more than halfway to the ceiling, and he started to spin and sway like a dead-weight pendulum. Automatically, he extended his hands in front of him.

"That'd be me, Pelvis," a voice below him cracked. "The stunt-master supreme." Somebody else was down there.

Elvis craned his head down to try to see who it was, but suddenly he was swinging so wildly and twirling so fast that his hands were no help in preventing him from colliding with the wall. First his right shoulder hit, then, careening back, his buttocks took a smack from the opposite wall, and spinning back again, his left hand scraped against a wood strut, grazing the skin on his knuckles. Along the way, the blond wig tumbled off his head and fell to the ground. In his gut, Elvis's anger was fighting with his fear, and his anger was winning hands down.

"Set me down! Now, man! *Now!*" Elvis bellowed.

"Say 'please,'" the new voice laughed.

The spinning started to slow, then the arc of the sway too, so that now Elvis was no longer bouncing against the walls. But he remained suspended a good six feet off the ground. He looked down. A muscular man in a black T-shirt and silky boxing trunks was gazing up at him with a supercilious grin on his face.

"Grieves, Mickey Grieves," the man said. "Pleasure to meet you, King."

Mickey Grieves, Squirm's good buddy who had advised him to use that stellar defense attorney, Regis Clifford. The man who then took the stand and accused Littlejon of not only being a murderer, but a rapist too. As Vernon liked to say, "With friends like these, who needs enemas?"

"Yes, I've heard about you, Grieves," Elvis said stonily. He felt like a real idiot still hanging up there—an idiot with enough fury in him to give Grieves a karate chop to the neck that would leave him with only one stunt left in his repertoire: drinking through a straw.

"Got a question for you, Pelvis," Grieves said in a mocking voice, scratching his head like he had a real stumper. "See, I can't carry a tune for the life of me, so I wouldn't think a minute of getting in front of a camera and wiggling my hips and singing about a hound dog. So what I'm wondering is, what in tarnation are you doing up there, Pelvis? I mean, I can't sing and you can't swing. See what I'm saying? You gotta stick to what you know and leave the rest alone, or you get yourself all tied up and hanging by your toes."

"Get me down now, Cathcart!" Elvis screamed.

In an instant, Elvis plummeted to the floor in a free fall, his legs splaying as he hit the gym mats, his left ankle twisting badly. He gained his footing and was seriously considering giving Grieves that chop he had promised himself when the ankle painfully buckled under him, dropping him to one knee. Grieves cackled like a coy-dog. Elvis lunged, grabbing the master stuntman just below the knees and throttling him hard to the ground. Grieves lay there stunned, the breath knocked out of him. And it was at that moment that two MGM security guards came dashing in through the stunt-shack door, one of them with his black baton raised, ready to knock heads. The two stood over Elvis and Grieves, staring down at them in utter bafflement.

"Mr. Presley, sir?" one of them said.

"We heard a scream," said the other.

"Get me out of here," Elvis barked. "I think I broke something."

His arms braced around the shoulders of the two security men, Elvis hopped out of the stunt shack on his right foot. He was fuming. But underneath his rage another feeling was emerging, a feeling that felt strangely consoling. For the first time in a long while, Elvis felt *one* pure emotion: hatred for Mickey Grieves.

8
A SLENDER HAIR

IT WASN'T a break, but it was a bad sprain. Bad enough to keep Elvis's ankle bound up and him on crutches for a week, the doctor at the MGM infirmary had said. But break or sprain, it wasn't any accident. Grieves had known exactly what he was doing. He must have been outside the shack the whole time Elvis was in there, must have heard Elvis quizzing Cathcart about Holly McDougal. No, it wasn't an accident, it was Grieves's threat: *Keep your nose out of this, Pelvis, or I'll leave you hanging by your toes!*

God knows, Grieves wouldn't be threatening Elvis if he wasn't somehow connected to the McDougal girl's murder. Maybe Grieves hadn't strangled the girl himself, but he surely knew who had. And the master stuntman wouldn't be messing with Elvis Presley if that person was only Squirm Littlejon. Man, it was a good thing the security guards had shown up when they did. One more minute and Elvis would have throttled Grieves by the neck and not let go until his hairy legs stopped twitching.

Joe and Joanie picked Elvis up at the studio and brought him back to Perugia Way and up to bed. He was spread out there now, Frederick Littlejon's trial transcript on one side of him and, on the other, a bag of White Tower two-bite burgers that they had picked up on the way home. The doctor had recommended a high-protein diet to help with the healing. Elvis popped an entire two-bite into his mouth and shifted onto his side. Man, that ankle ached. The doc had given him some pills for the pain, but Elvis decided to hold off for a while. He wanted to read with a clear head:

The State of California v Frederick Littlejon, Esquire

Elvis had to smile at that. It was probably the one and only time in his life that Squirm had an "Esquire" appended to his name.

The charge was first-degree murder, nothing about rape in the indictment. A total of twenty-two witnesses were listed on the first page, all but three of them for the prosecution. Four of the prosecution witnesses were forensic experts, three of them professors at UCLA, the fourth imported from Harvard Law School. Only one of the defense witnesses was a forensic expert: a man named Hector Garcia from the Instituto Tecnológico Autónomo de México. That Regis Clifford sure knew how to pick them.

Elvis turned to the prosecution's opening statement:

MR. L. CLIFFORD: Ladies and Gentlemen of the jury. We have the unpleasant task today of contemplating the murder of a beautiful young woman, ruthlessly strangled in the prime of her life by a vicious and cowardly man, Fred Littlejon. . . .

Mr. L. *Clifford*? Elvis flipped back to the first page of the transcript and looked at the bottom:

FOR THE PROSECUTION: Mr. LeRoy Clifford, Esquire, First Assistant District Attorney.

FOR THE DEFENSE: Mr. Regis Clifford, Esquire, Attorney at Law.

Elvis picked up the phone off the bed table and dialed Regis's number. This time it only rang twice before he picked up.

"The offices of Regis Clifford," the attorney said brightly. What a difference ten hours and six hundred dollars made.

"It's Tatum," Elvis said.

"Oh, Tatum," Clifford said. Elvis could literally hear the air of deflation gush out of him. "I'm sorry, Mr. Tatum, but I never got out to East L.A. today. Prior commitments. But I'm only charging you for a half day. . . . Listen, could you hold the wire a second? I've got something on the stove."

There was no stove in Clifford's office.

"No, I can't hold," Elvis said curtly. "I need to know something right now. Who was the prosecutor in the Littlejon case?"

"Let me see," the attorney mumbled. "It's been a while, uh—"

"Clifford," Elvis snapped. "LeRoy Clifford."

"Right."

"Like your name."

"It's a common name," Regis said. "Irish, you know. We're all over the place."

"Is he any relation to you?" Elvis asked.

"Who?"

"For godssake, *LeRoy Clifford*. Is he any relation to you?"

No response while the attorney for the defense lit a cigarette and noisily inhaled several times.

"He was," Regis said finally.

"Was?"

"We've been estranged for years, Mr. Tatum," Clifford said, once again attempting to hide behind a voice loaded with upper-class cadences.

"Who is he, Clifford?" Elvis barked into the phone.

"My brother," he answered quietly. "My twin brother."

"God Almighty! Isn't that illegal or something? The two of you on opposite sides of the same case?"

"Nothing illegal about it," Clifford answered. "As long as we didn't share any privileged information. And there was no danger of that. We don't even speak to each other, not even at discovery."

Elvis shook his head incredulously. "Why didn't you tell me that this morning, Clifford?"

"It didn't seem relevant."

"Not relevant to tell me that you lost this case to your own kin? Your own *twin brother*?"

"It wasn't the first time I lost to him, Mr. Presley," Regis Clifford said.

Elvis shot straight up in his bed. "What did you just call me?"

"Mr. Presley," Clifford said. "I don't know you well enough to call you Elvis."

"You know who I am."

"I may have the occasional drink, Mr. Presley, but I am not unconscious," Clifford said.

"Why didn't you mention *that* before?" Elvis asked.

"You introduced yourself as Tatum, I called you Tatum," Clifford replied. Not a bad answer, actually. "In other words, it didn't seem relevant, Mr. Presley," he went on airily, clearly pleased with himself.

"We need to talk, Clifford," Elvis said.

"We are talking."

"In person," Elvis blurted out. "Tonight."

"It's eight o'clock."

"One of the advantages of doing business with you is you're open night and day," Elvis said.

"Touché," Clifford said. "I'll leave a candle burning in the window for you."

"It'll have to be at my place. I've got a little problem," Elvis said. "Take a cab. You haven't made a dent in today's expenses yet. And Clifford?"

"What, Mr. Presley?"

"I keep a dry house here."

"I'll manage," Clifford replied. Elvis gave him the address and they hung up.

Elvis's head was spinning. That morning, Clifford had said that everybody has a twin out there doing the exact opposite of what he is doing. He'd added some poetry about "cosmic balance," but he'd actually meant it as a matter of raw fact—he and his twin, LeRoy, had been out there on the exact opposite sides of the Littlejon case.

Elvis popped the final two White Tower burgers into his mouth, one after another, and turned back to the trial transcript. First Assistant District Attorney LeRoy Clifford had laid out his case methodically, starting with the two cops who were the first at the scene of the crime after receiving a tip-off from an anonymous phone caller. The policemen not only described the crime scene, but produced several large glossy photographs of it that were passed to the jury and entered into evidence as exhibits.

But no one had mentioned the phone tip to Elvis before. Had they tried to trace the call? Elvis flipped to Regis's cross-examination of the two policemen. He did ask about the call, but no, they didn't have a clue who it was from and they had not traced it. All they could say was that it was a woman's voice. On redirect, LeRoy got the cops to recite some stock sermon about the importance of protecting anonymous informants lest they hold back information out of fear of reprisal. In other words, tracing the call wouldn't have been the decent thing to do.

Next came the prosecution's three forensic specialists, a triple threat with triple evidence: Littlejon's fingerprints were all over the girl's belongings and there were some on her person; they'd also lifted clear prints from the rubber tubbing she'd been garroted with; and they had swabs that proved she had engaged in sexual intercourse shortly before her murder. On cross, Regis had asked the obvious question: Were there anyone else's prints on McDougal's possessions and body? The experts had replied almost off-handedly that, of course, there were other fingerprints, there are on almost everything and everybody at any given time, but most of those other prints were faint or smudged, suggesting that they had been imprinted less vigorously and undoubtedly earlier in the day.

MR. R. CLIFFORD: Let me get this straight, Professor. What you are saying, essentially, is that the person who leaves the clearest fingerprints wins the prize—that prize being a murder indictment.

PROFESSOR G. GILMARTIN: That is not what I am saying at all, Counselor.

MR. R. CLIFFORD: Funny, that's how it sounded to me.

MR. L. CLIFFORD: Objection, Your Honor. Harassing the witness.

JUDGE LOWENSTEIN: Sustained.

Elvis smiled. He didn't know whether or not Regis had been tanked at the trial, but right there he certainly sounded a whole lot more intelligent than anybody else did.

Regis had then asked Professor Gilmartin if the swabs proved that it was definitely Littlejon who had engaged in intercourse with the victim. No, Gilmartin admitted, but there was other physical evidence that did, namely several strands of pubic hair that matched Littlejon's.

MR. R. CLIFFORD: Excuse me, Professor, but this is one of those many things I don't know a thing about. How do you go about matching pubic hairs?

PROFESSOR G. GILMARTIN: A series of tests for density, size, tensile strength, and color.

MR. R. CLIFFORD: Really? And there's that much difference between one person's little pubic hair and another person's?

PROFESSOR G. GILMARTIN: There are significant differences, yes.

MR. R. CLIFFORD: So, if we could pluck one pubic hair from each person in this courtroom—with their permission, of course—

[Vocal Disruption: Laughter.]

JUDGE LOWENSTEIN: Order. Order in the courtroom.

MR. R. CLIFFORD: As I was saying, under those circumstances, would you be able to go around and match each hair to its original, uh, site?

[Vocal Disruption: Laughter.]

JUDGE LOWENSTEIN: Order, please.

PROFESSOR G. GILMARTIN: We certainly would be able to make a match by groups.

MR. R. CLIFFORD: Groups? How many groups would that be, Professor?

PROFESSOR G. GILMARTIN: If one calculates all the permutations—as I say, for density, size, tensile strength, and color—that would come to twelve clearly discernible groups.

MR. R. CLIFFORD: Twelve? You mean every twelfth person essentially has the same pubic hair?

PROFESSOR G. GILMARTIN: You could put it that way if you like.

MR. R. CLIFFORD: Gosh, Professor, that sure seems like a slender piece of hair to hang a man on.

Man, that Regis had a mouth on him! But what was he getting at? Littlejon had admitted that he'd had sex with the McDougal girl that afternoon.

LeRoy Clifford had then trotted out one character witness after another—half of them MGM employees and most of those Littlejon's fellow stuntmen. All their stories were pretty much the same: Holly McDougal was the closest thing to an angel they'd ever met, and Fredrick "Squirm" Littlejon had all the markings of a creep and scoundrel, not to mention a pervert.

Mickey Grieves had been the last called to the stand, and he was a real prize. The man probably took acting lessons—heck, everybody else out here did—because the words came out of him in dramatic, writerly sentences. Miss McDougal was "a tender soul, like a delicate flower." And Littlejon was known as Squirm because of his sneakiness; he was "a snake in the grass with a venomous bite." There was no way Mickey Grieves could have composed those lines, let alone composed them on the spot. Finally came Grieves's corker: he figured Littlejon had raped the girl and then murdered her when she threatened to turn him in. Grieves's evidence was a supposed conversation he had had with the accused in which Littlejon had bragged about raping several underage girls. Regis had objected on the grounds that this was only hearsay evidence and the judge concurred but, of course, the damage was done—done and dirty.

On cross, Regis had started with, "Was it true that Grieves himself had engaged in sexual congress with the victim on numerous occasions?"

M. GRIEVES: I deeply resent that question, Counselor. Holly was a child the age of my own daughter. I am not a child molester, sir.

R. CLIFFORD: But, at the time, you didn't know her true age, isn't that a fact? She was passing herself as eighteen, wasn't she?

M. GRIEVES: Well, that's pretty darn young in my book.

R. CLIFFORD: What I don't understand, Mr. Grieves, is how it is that every one of you stuntman knew Miss McDougal so well. I mean, she was just another bit player out of hundreds of bit players on the MGM lot.

M. GRIEVES: Holly—Miss McDougal—just kinda took a shine to us. And us to her. Stunt people are a friendly bunch, for the most part. Mostly cowboys and rodeo folk, family people, don't you know. And I know Holly didn't have a daddy of her own, not living at home, at least. So I guess we were kind of family to her. Substitute daddies, you might say.

The creep was going for an Oscar.

Strangely, the prosecution had not called Nanette Poulette, aka Nancy Pollard, to the stand. How could that be? Regis had labeled her the most damning witness of them all, and considering Grieves's choice testimony, she must of have been a humdinger.

The answer was on the next page of the transcript. Poulette/Pollard was the first witness for the *defense*. But after a couple of exchanges with Littlejon's beloved fiancée, Regis asked the judge to have her declared a hostile witness.

Hostile was too kind a word for the job Poulette did on Squirm. According to her, Littlejon was a pervert of the lowest order. She immediately launched into a detailed description of his dress-up games and spankings, and then, for a capper, she said that during these sick encounters he had insisted on calling her "Holly." Like Regis said, Poulette had handed the jury the keys to the California Correctional Institution on a silver platter.

Regis's next witness wasn't hostile, just dense. His name was Jerry Griswold and he'd been the crane operator for Squirm's stunt on *The Honeymoon Machine* on the day of the murder. Griswold confirmed that they'd had harness trouble on the set, which left Littlejon dangling at sixteen feet for several hours. Elvis had no trouble picturing that. Just reading about it made his ribs ache and his ankle throb even worse. Then, without being prompted, Griswold began rattling on about how weird Squirm had acted while he was hanging up there—doing circus tricks and cracking dumb jokes and telling everybody that he was Harry Houdini reincarnated.

> J. GRISWOLD: He said, like, *Look at me everybody. I can slip out of anything.*

Little doubt that, at this point, the jury thought this was Littlejon's way of saying he could even slip out of a murder wrap.

Regis's next witness was Dr. Hector Garcia of the Instituto Tecnológico Autónomo de México. The transcript recorded that the court stenographer had requested that the name of the instituto be spelled out letter by letter, a laborious process that consumed almost an entire page. It got worse. Garcia had to repeat every one of his responses four or five times because the judge insisted that his accent was impenetrable. Finally, a translator had been summoned, and Dr. Garcia was instructed to give his testimony in Spanish. That sure must have impressed the jury—an expert witness who couldn't even speak English.

But, in whatever language, Elvis found Dr. Hector Garcia's testimony riveting. Regis did not ask Garcia anything about the murder itself, only about the evidence of Holly's sexual activity. The Mexican doctor explained that he had been granted permission to take his own swabs of Miss McDougal's vaginal canal, that he had then refrigerated the samples and transported them to his own laboratory in Santa Teresa. There, using a technique that he had recently developed, he suspended the samples in a neutral medium and spun the resulting mixture in a centrifuge. This process resulted in two samples, one slightly but distinctly denser than the other. Garcia had then spread a micro-thin layer of each of the new samples on glass slides, stained them, and then inspected each under an electron microscope. This, too, was a new technique of his own devising. What it revealed was that the victim had engaged in sexual intercourse with *two* different men within a period of five to seven hours.

> R. CLIFFORD: Dr. Garcia, in layman's terms, can you tell the court how you were able to reach this conclusion?
>
> H. GARCIA (VIA INTERPRETER, M. SANCHEZ): Human spermatozoa contains one half of the blueprint of a potential embryo in the form of individual genes and chromosomes. Each set is different—which, of course, is why one man's child looks different from another's. We have no idea what particular chromosome results in what particular human characteristic or phenotype. But under an electron microscope, they certainly can look very different from one another. And that is what I saw: traces of chromosomes from two very different donors.
>
> R. CLIFFORD: Could it not have been chromosomes from two different emissions from the same man?
>
> H. GARCIA (VIA INTERPRETER, M. SANCHEZ): That's highly unlikely. The markers I saw were remarkably different from one another.

R. CLIFFORD: Dr. Garcia, again, in layman's terms, can you tell the court how you ascertained that one of these emissions was deposited five to seven hours after the first?

H. GARCIA (VIA INTERPRETER, M. SANCHEZ): Spermatozoa are like little tadpoles propelled by the movement of their tails. They begin to die almost immediately and this is reflected in their motility—how fast and vigorously they swim. In effect, I was able to determine that one set of sperm was approximately five to seven hours further along in this process than the other.

Regis had then gotten Garcia to repeat the whole business in even simpler terms to make sure that the jury got the main point: *On the day she was killed, Holly McDougal had had sexual relations with two different men at two different times.*

LeRoy Clifford had immediately asked for a short recess before he began his cross-examination of Garcia. From his questions that followed, it was clear that he spent that recess huddled with his own forensic team.

L. CLIFFORD: Dr. Garcia, we have with us in this courtroom four of the most prominent forensic specialists in the United States. And yet not one of them has heard of the procedure you described. How would you account for that?

H. GARCIA (VIA INTERPRETER, M. SANCHEZ): That is not for me to say, is it? But the procedure is very new, and perhaps my learned colleagues in the United States are not completely up to date on procedures developed in other countries. Perhaps they have not read my articles about it in Mexico's *Journal of Forensic Medicine*.

L. CLIFFORD: Excuse me, Dr. Garcia, but in what language is that journal written?

H. GARCIA (VIA INTERPRETER, M. SANCHEZ): Spanish, of course. It is the language of my country. But I, myself, read all of the forensic journals in German, French, and English.

L. CLIFFORD: English, eh? A language in which you appear to have severely limited proficiency.

R. CLIFFORD: Objection, Your Honor. Harassing the witness.

JUDGE LOWENSTEIN: Overruled.

H. GARCIA (VIA INTERPRETER, M. SANCHEZ): Reading and speaking are two different skills, sir. I have no problem reading medical journals in English.

L. CLIFFORD: Really? How would you ever be able to know that, Doctor?

R. CLIFFORD: Objection, Your Honor. Harassing the witness.

JUDGE LOWENSTEIN: Overruled.

Elvis felt his blood boil. What Assistant District Attorney LeRoy Clifford was saying in no uncertain terms—and he was getting away with it—is that only a fool would take the word of a dumb Mexican who can barely speak English. And then LeRoy had gone in for the kill.

L. CLIFFORD: Do you believe it is possible to match a particular sperm sample to a particular donor?

H. GARCIA (VIA INTERPRETER, M. SANCHEZ): Yes, I do. But I am pretty much alone in this belief at this time. I have no doubt that in the future my findings will be borne out by other scientists.

[Vocal Disruption: Laughter.]

JUDGE LOWENSTEIN: Doctors, please.

Apparently, it was the eminences from Harvard and UCLA who had cracked up at Garcia's scientific prediction. Obviously, professional respect did not cross borders, particularly the one to the south.

Regis's final witness was the defendant himself, and it was a disaster from start to finish. It was not that Squirm did not give the right answers or that he was inconsistent on cross-examination, it was that the proceedings had to be halted seven separate times for the defendant to regain his composure. As the court stenographer deftly put it: "F. Littlejon: [Inaudible; sobbing.]" It seems F. Littlejon weeped and wailed virtually every time Nanette Poulette's name was mentioned. On the witness stand, Squirm was about the furthest thing there was from the slippery Harry Houdini.

The jury deliberated for exactly one hour, the minimum set by Judge Lowenstein. Frederick Littlejon, Esquire, was found guilty of murder in the first degree.

Elvis shuffled the pages of the transcript together and put them back in the folder. Only then did he realize just how much his ankle was killing him. He reached for the vial of painkillers on his bed table and popped one into his mouth.

9
THE UNIVERSAL THEMES OF ROCK AND ROLL

A FAINT rolling drumbeat. Or was it the summer rain pattering on the roof of his Tupelo bedroom? A soothing rhythm, like the bass and drum intro to an Italian ballad about love and loss and the hope for a new beginning. He could almost hear the lyric.

"Elvis?"

Yes, the lyric was coming now, although it was not in English or Italian or Spanish or any other language he'd ever heard of. It was a lyric that rose above any man-made language into the universal language of the human soul. Words that were not *about* feelings, but were the feelings themselves—the aches and sweet yearnings of every man who ever longed to love with a pure heart.

"Elvis?"

He opened his eyes. Someone was rapping rhythmically on his bedroom door. He was still sitting up in bed, the transcript folder on one side of him and the empty White Tower bag on the other. He looked at his watch: 9:10. If he had slept, it could only have been for a few minutes, but he felt like he was coming out of a long, deep sleep.

"Who's there?"

"It's me, Elvis." Joe's voice. "Got a man here who said you sent for him. A Mr. Regis Clifford."

"Thanks, Joe. Let him in."

Clifford had dressed up for the occasion in a three-piece charcoal-gray suit, white shirt, and paisley silk tie, and he'd combed his sandy hair straight back with the benefit of Brylcreem.

"Good evening, Mr. Presley," he said, striding to the bed and shaking Elvis's hand. "Sorry to hear about your mishap."

Except for the Scotch on his breath, you would have thought Regis was the Prince of Wales. Heck, for all Elvis knew, the Prince of Wales smelled of Scotch too.

"Want me to bring you anything, Elvis?" Joe asked. "Joanie could fix you up some cocoa."

"No thanks, Joe," Elvis said. He turned to Regis. "How about you, Mr. Clifford? Cocoa?"

Clifford made a big show of considering the offer, then smiled and said, "It just doesn't feel like a cocoa kind of evening, if you know what I mean."

As soon as Joe left, Regis pulled a chair up alongside Elvis's bed and looked at him seriously. "How did it happen?" he asked, gesturing at Elvis's ankle.

Elvis told him.

"Son of a bitch," Regis said. "Grieves would string up his mother if it suited his purposes."

For a brief moment, Elvis thought he heard that wordless lyric again. It was like a siren song in those Greek stories that Selma had read to him one evening. The song wanted to pull him away from this world.

"And what do you suppose his purposes are?" Elvis said finally.

"To scare you off, I imagine," Regis said. "Although it seems like an awfully clumsy way to go about it. Especially considering your personal stature. You wouldn't think a lowly stuntman would risk offending the most valuable star on the studio's roster. Seems like a guaranteed way to lose his job."

"I hadn't thought of that," Elvis said.

"So, *are* you going to tell MGM to fire him?"

"No," Elvis said. "I think I want to keep Grieves right there, where I can keep an eye on him."

"And where he can keep an eye on you," Regis said. "Let's hope it's just an eye."

Elvis nodded, then picked up the transcript folder and pulled out the pages.

"I read it through, Regis," he said, "and I don't know much about these things, but it seems to me you did a pretty decent job of defending Squirm, considering."

"Thank you, Mr. Presley." Clifford seemed a lot more gratified by this compliment than Elvis would have expected.

"Why don't you call me, Elvis?"

"It certainly suits you better than 'Jodie' does," Regis said, smiling.

"I'd like to talk to Dr. Hector Garcia," Elvis said. "In person."

"I think it can be arranged," Regis replied.

"Down there in Mexico," Elvis continued. "At his laboratory. See how he does his little procedure."

"Okay, Elvis," Regis said. He hesitated a second, then, "Would you want me to come with you? I, uh, I *am* fluent in Spanish."

"Sounds like a good idea then," Elvis said. "Make the date and I'll have someone get us the plane tickets."

"Maybe it would be best if I took care of that part too," Regis said. "You probably don't want the people around you knowing what you're up to, at least until we know who you can trust in this enterprise."

As if on cue, there was another knock at Elvis's door.

"I'm kinda busy, Joe," Elvis said.

"Not Joe—it's me." The dulcet tones of Colonel Thomas Parker.

Instinctively, Elvis shoved the trial transcript under a pillow. "Come on in, Colonel."

Parker burst through the door like somebody had shoved him from behind. "Who the hell did this to you?" was his greeting.

"Did it to myself, Tom," Elvis replied. "I should've heeded your warning about trying to do stunts myself."

"What stunts, boy? We're all done shooting that picture."

"Just fooling around on the lot," Elvis said. Man, he was getting awful tired of the Colonel treating him like some truant schoolboy, even if he was lying to him like a schoolboy just now.

"And who's this? Your doctor?" Parker glared at Clifford.

"No, sir, I'm Mr. Presley's—"

"My scriptwriter," Elvis blurted, not knowing where that came from. Lately, he seemed to have developed a genuine talent for flip-flopping people's identities. Maybe he had learned something after all from playing two roles in *Kissin' Cousins*.

"Scriptwriter?" Parker bellowed.

"That's right," Regis jumped in. "We're developing quite an interesting property for Mr. Presley. Something that touches on the universal themes of love and betrayal."

Elvis struggled to keep from grinning. Man, that Regis had a mouth and a half on him.

"Well, I sure as hell hope it's something he can play on crutches," Parker snapped back.

"Now there's a brilliant touch," Regis replied sarcastically. Elvis was beginning to realize that one big problem with Regis Clifford is that he never knew when to stop.

"How long are you going to be laid up, son?" Parker said, suddenly sounding genuinely concerned—although his chief concern was undoubtedly Elvis's schedule.

"Just a week," Elvis answered.

"Well, that's not too bad," Parker said. "But maybe you should be in a hospital where they can look after you properly."

"I'm fine here, Tom," Elvis said.

"Well, since you're going to have a little time on your hands, I brought you some reading matter." Parker signaled to Joe in the doorway who promptly lugged in a peach crate full of scripts. And then another and another. After the final one had been set against the bedroom wall, the Colonel turned to Clifford and said, "No offense intended, of course, Mr. Screenwriter. But there just might be something in there with the universal themes of rock and roll."

Parker touched Elvis in the middle of his forehead with his forefinger, like some kind of benediction, and started to leave, but then he abruptly turned to one of the crates and lifted off a small soft package covered with butcher's paper and tied with string. He set it on Elvis's bed.

"Almost forgot," he said. "This came in for you just as I was leaving the studio. Has 'personal' written on it and you know how I respect those things." Then he left, closing the door behind him.

Elvis held his hand over his mouth for as long as he could, but then he couldn't hold it back any longer: he burst out laughing. Laughed so hard that he was popping up and down on the bed-springs. And pretty soon, Regis was laughing along with him just from the sheer infectiousness of it.

"Th. . . that man," Elvis sputtered through his laughter. "If he ain't the devil himself, he surely is his warm-up act. The devil's own comedian."

Regis took out his handkerchief and patted his mouth. "Perhaps I should be leaving now too," he said.

"Not yet, Regis," Elvis said. "There's something I need to ask you about. It's the reason I wanted to see you tonight—you know, face-to-face. You see, I've got this picture in my mind of you and your brother in that courtroom. You're identical, right? Now how the heck did that look to everybody? I mean, it must've been confusing for the jury and all."

Regis took his time doing more work on his face with the handkerchief. Finally, he said, "LeRoy and I don't really look that much alike. Not since we were kids."

"How's that? The way you dress and wear your hair? That kind of thing?"

Regis walked over to the window opposite the bed and looked out. "I sure could use a little nip about now," he said, his back turned.

"Sorry, Regis. Like I told you, I keep a dry house here," Elvis said.

"I, uh, I brought a flask with me," Regis murmured, his back still to Elvis.

"Do what you got to do, Regis," Elvis said. "But it can't be good for you."

Regis swiftly withdrew a flat silver flask from the inside pocket of his suit jacket, screwed off the top, and drained the contents in two swallows. Again, he took out his handkerchief and mopped around his mouth, then returned to the side of Elvis's bed and sat down.

"LeRoy's face is deformed," he said quietly. "Misshapen."

"Born that way?"

"No," Regis said. "He had an accident. When he was ten years old. BB gun accident that blew out his right eye and took a piece of his cheekbone with it."

"God Almighty!"

"So people do not have any problem telling us apart," Regis went on. "The left side of LeRoy's face looks just like mine. But on the other, he's a freak, a freak with a glass eye that wanders and a cheek that turns in where it should turn out."

"That is an awful thing," Elvis murmured.

"Indeed it is," Regis said. "Especially considering the fact that I did it."

"What?"

"I pulled the trigger," Regis said evenly. "I shot my brother in the face."

Elvis put both of his hands flat against his face. His fingers were trembling. "It . . . It was an accident, right?" he blurted out.

"Maybe."

"What in God's name do you mean, *'maybe'*?" Elvis stared at Regis.

Regis bowed his head. "It seemed like an accident at the time," he said in a monotone. "And that is the way it was written up, of course. Couple kids fooling around with a BB gun, shooting at pop bottles out by the lake, taking turns, passing the gun back and forth. And then, this one time, LeRoy passes it to me and—*Pop!*—it goes off in his face just as I grab it."

"Then it *was* an accident," Elvis said.

Regis raised his head and looked solemnly into Elvis's eyes. "Have you ever read any Sigmund Freud?" he asked.

"Heard of him, never read him," Elvis answered.

"Well, Dr. Freud says that there are no accidents. Things may seem like an accident, but there is always a human motive hidden there somewhere. An unconscious motive—the kind that secretly wants to blow your brother's head off."

"That's crazy," Elvis said.

"It sounds that way, doesn't it?" Regis said. "But it's funny the way people just naturally find their way around to that point of view. Maybe that part is unconscious too."

"Who are you talking about?"

"My parents, for one," Regis said. "They kept assuring me it was just an accident and that I shouldn't feel guilty about it. But the more they said that to me, the more I knew that they were thinking just the opposite. That I had ruined my brother's life because I was careless. And, little by little, it wasn't because I was careless—it was because I was *bad*."

"They said that?"

"Of course not. They never said anything like that. They just lived it. And so that's how I became Bad Regis, the proverbial evil twin," Clifford went on with a grim smile. "You know how you never want to disappoint your parents' expectations of you? Well, I didn't want to disappoint mine. No, sir, from that day on I fulfilled theirs. Got expelled from school that year. The first of many schools, I might add. Arrested for shoplifting at the age of twelve. Off to military academy where they threw me out for shouting obscenities in chapel. Ran away to Mexico when I was fifteen. Worked in a furniture factory there for close to a year. My little twist on migrant labor."

"But you went to college. Became a lawyer," Elvis said.

"After a fashion," Regis replied. "That part still amazes me. Maybe it's genetic. My father was a lawyer and a judge, and his father before him. Naturally, they went to Stanford and Harvard Law. I, myself, took a slightly different route. Sent myself through night school by tending bar. Took me almost ten years, but here I am, Counselor Regis Clifford, Attorney at Law."

"And LeRoy?"

"It took over a year for LeRoy to heal," Regis said. "They did some reconstructive surgery on him, put in the glass eye, but it never completely worked. He'd look fairly decent for a few months, but then the right side of his face would simply cave in."

"Awful."

"Yes, awful," Regis said. "That's what LeRoy sees every day when he looks in the mirror. And, when he looks at me, he sees the face he should have had."

"But he became a lawyer too," Elvis said.

"That's right. Stanford, Harvard, Assistant District Attorney, and now he's got the family seat on the state supreme court. I saved the powers that be a lot of trouble by eliminating myself from the competition for the Clifford judgeship."

Elvis shook his head slowly. "So, when you look at LeRoy, you see the man *you* could have been."

Regis chortled. "You know, Elvis, for a rock and roll singer, you have one hell of a dangerous mind."

"Maybe that's what it takes," Elvis answered, smiling. "Danger is one of the universal themes of rock and roll, don't ya know?"

Both men laughed, then Regis stood, yawning.

"We'll have to continue this seminar some other time, Elvis," he said. "Unless you feel like having me for a bedmate."

"You're not my type, Regis," Elvis said, grinning.

"Well, you sure are a good-looking fella, but you're not mine either." Regis started to extend his hand to Elvis, but then his hand abruptly took a detour and picked up the bottle of painkillers off of the bed table. He brought it up to his eyes. "Codeine, eh? Marvelous stuff."

"It's for my ankle," Elvis said.

"Oh, it kills the pain all right. *All* of it. Now there's an idea for a song, Elvis—what a man's willing to do to feel no pain." Regis set the bottle back down and straightened up. He looked solemnly at Elvis for a moment before he went on. "You know that business about there not being any accidents?"

Elvis nodded.

"I believe it," Regis said quietly. "Deep down, I believe it." After Regis had gone, Elvis sat very still in his bed for several minutes. A distressing thought was tugging at his consciousness—not a fully-formed thought, just the embryo of one. He reached for the bottle of painkillers and popped another tablet in his mouth. It was not long before he heard that siren song again.

10
BLUE SUEDE SCHMOOZE

THE sleep of the blessed—that's what Mamma used to call it. One of those deep-down slumbers that is not even interrupted by a dream. It was almost eleven when Elvis woke, and his first thought was that there was something to be said for sleeping alone. This had been the first night that week that he hadn't slept with Priscilla at his side. Even in his sleep, he had known she was there, tempting him, troubling him.

Instead of Priscilla, on the pillow next to his was that paper-wrapped package Colonel had left for him. The string slipped off easily. Inside was the Jodie Tatum blond wig and a piece of notepaper. Elvis unfolded it:

Dear Mr. Presley,
I kannut tell you how bad I feel about today. I respek you more than any other man and I shuda known better. I got things to tell you, important things. Doin a rodeo out near Reno tomorow and the nex day. But maybe we kin talk after.

Respekly, Will Cathcart

P.S. You dropt this.
P.P.S. It weren't no accident.

Elvis tossed the wig to the end of his bed. No, Will, it wasn't an accident. There *are* no accidents.

Elvis swung his legs over the side of the bed, setting his left foot down lightly. The ankle still hurt plenty, a tingling sensation now added to the throbbing. For a moment, he considered taking another one of the painkillers, but that wouldn't do. He had places to go and things to do.

He rang up Joanie on the intercom and asked her to bring up some coffee and a piece of toast. He didn't have much of a hunger this morning—maybe because those White Tower two-bites were still taking up so much space. He also asked Joanie if she could bring up those crutches that the MGM doctor had given him.

"You aren't getting up today?" Joanie said. It was more of a statement than a question.

"Just a little," Elvis replied.

"I don't think that's wise, Elvis."

"Probably not," Elvis said. "Put a little jam on that toast, would you, Joanie?"

Elvis ate and dressed quickly. He tried to put a shoe on his left foot, but between the swelling and the bandaging it wouldn't go on, so he just slipped a second sock over the first. Then he called Joe and asked him to bring the car around front—he had a meeting at MGM in twenty minutes. The crutches were more hindrance than help negotiating the stairs, so Elvis just hung on to the banister with both hands and hopped down sideways. Joanie watched him, wagging her head like a Tennessee nanny.

"No need to look so grim, girl," Elvis said, smiling. "Just call me Hopalong Presley."

Their car had scarcely made the turn onto Sepulveda Boulevard when Elvis saw a blue Volkswagen Beetle cut in just behind them. He had first spotted that Beetle in his side mirror back by Holmby Park, weaving in and out behind them. Now he turned in his seat and looked back through the rear window at the car. A gaunt man with a gray beard and a black knit cap was driving, and he glared back at Elvis with a mean-looking squint.

"Think we're being followed," Elvis said, turning forward again.

"Autograph seeker?" Joe said, glancing in his rearview mirror.

"Don't think so."

"What then?"

"Don't know, Joe. But let's lose him, okay?"

Joe screwed up his face. "What the heck for, Elvis?"

"Just do it!" Elvis snapped.

Joe shook his head a couple of times, then gunned it. He jerked the Eldorado into the left lane, then gunned it more. They were flying. A mile later, Joe slipped back into the right lane, then cut off sharply onto the access road to the Mountaingate Country Club. There, he slowed down to thirty. Elvis looked in the side mirror. No Beetle in sight. He reached over and touched Joe's sleeve.

"Sorry I spoke harshly," he said.

"You're just twitchy from your accident," Joe said.

"That's right, Joey."

Elvis hobbled on his crutches into Nancy Pollard's office almost an hour late. Her assistant, Miss Aronson, a petite bleached blonde of indeterminate age—somewhere between twenty-five and forty—greeted him at the door with a bubbly, "I put the ribs on the hot plate to keep them warm."

"Forgive me for being so late, ma'am," Elvis said.

"We're glad you made it at all, considering your awful accident." This from a willowy redhead in a tailored pink silk pants suit as she strode from her office with her hand extended. "Nancy Pollard. It's a great honor to meet you, Mr. Presley."

Elvis managed to shake her hand with the crutch still tucked under his right shoulder. "So you heard about my little fall," Elvis said.

"Of course, Mr. Presley," Pollard said. "It's the talk of the campus." She leaned her pert face close to his and smiled coquettishly. "There's even talk that you are going to sue us for gazillions of dollars for neglect or something."

"Not likely," Elvis said.

Pollard led Elvis into her office where Aronson was already busily portioning out baby back ribs, little squares of corn bread, and mounds of coleslaw onto gold-flecked French bone china. The ribs looked like beef jerky. The china looked downright embarrassed.

"Well, I cannot tell you how privileged I feel," Pollard said, tucking a linen napkin onto her lap. "It isn't often we're able to go right to the source. Skip the middlemen with all their preconceived ideas and work with the one person who knows what's best for him. For *you*, Mr. Presley."

It was obviously a prepared little speech, but Pollard delivered it well, complete with sincere nods and a modest smile. Then again, she had put in time as an actress, including one consummate performance on the witness stand.

Elvis poked at a rib with his fork. If it had been at all moist before being rewarmed on the hot plate, it now had the consistency of a horse whip. He moved his fork over to the coleslaw. What in tarnation were those ant-looking things swimming around in it?

"Caraway seeds," Aronson piped up behind him. She had remained standing, the attentive waitress anticipating his every question. "It's a California touch."

Elvis nodded. He set down his fork.

"Let me tell you what I've been thinking about, Miss Pollard," he began. "I want to dig into a drama that has universal themes. Say, love and betrayal."

"Interesting," Pollard said.

"Yes, very," Aronson echoed.

"Like, what if I was this fella who was happily married," Elvis continued. "A regular guy with a regular job. And a nice-looking woman for a wife, but regular too."

"Tuesday Weld," Aronson murmured.

"Perhaps," Pollard said.

"Well, a Tuesday Weld type," Aronson countered.

"And then, one day, I—this fella—gets into some kind of trouble," Elvis went on. "Maybe with the law or something like that. But my wife, this woman I have loved and cherished with all my heart, she suddenly turns against me."

Pollard set down her fork and dabbed at her mouth with her napkin.

"How?" she asked. "How does she turn against you?"

"Well, maybe she decides on her own that I am guilty of this trouble I got into, whatever it is," Elvis said, looking directly into Pollard's pale eyes. "And not only that, she, like, goes to the police and tells them she's got evidence to prove I'm guilty."

"Classic," Aronson said, breathlessly. "Really, it's like a Greek drama."

Pollard pushed her plate away and busied herself for several seconds with meticulously folding up her napkin.

"And *are* you guilty?" she asked finally, looking steadily back at Elvis.

"No," Elvis said. "I am not."

Pollard leaned across the table toward Elvis, those sincere nods and modest smiles in action again.

"But wouldn't it be more dramatically interesting if you *were* guilty," she said. "Then your wife would be caught in a fascinating moral dilemma. Should she go with her loyalty to you, the man she loves? Or should she go with honesty? She really struggles with it. I mean, she loves you dearly, but she's a good Christian woman who truly believes in right and wrong. And, in the end, she decides to sacrifice her love for you to this higher good."

"I like that," Aronson said emphatically. "Lots of texture there." She had begun clearing the plates off the table; neither Elvis nor Pollard had taken a bite.

"But let's say I'm not guilty," Elvis said flatly. "And then we've got ourselves a real mystery story—who did commit this crime I'm accused of?"

Pollard sat up straight and leaned her head way back, her long red hair hanging dramatically behind her. She was a good-looking woman all right, but Elvis could see why she'd never made it big as an actress: she had a real affinity for the overplayed gesture.

"Motive," Pollard said softly, staring at the ceiling. "What could your wife's motive possibly be if you actually are innocent?"

"I don't know," Elvis said. "Maybe she never really loved me. Maybe she was in love with somebody else the whole time and I just didn't realize it, seeing as I was blinded by my own love for her."

Pollard shook her head, a simper curling her thin lips. "Forgive me, Mr. Presley, but that sounds a bit trite. More like an afternoon soap opera than a major motion picture."

"Wait a sec," Aronson said, halting at the door with the full plates balanced in both hands. "Let's stick with that a moment. Say the wife's in love with somebody else, and she and this guy want to get rid of the husband. So they set him up—frame him for some crime. And *that's* why she goes to the police with the damning evidence."

"That's only been done about a gazillion times," Pollard said wearily. Then, "But, thank you, Maryjane. Please close the door after you."

The moment Aronson shut the door, Pollard rose and strode around the table until she was standing next to Elvis's chair. She grasped one of the crutches he had leaned against the table and balanced it on its tip between the two of them, playfully catching it every time it started to topple, then balancing it again.

"I get the impression that there is something you want to say to me, Mr. Presley," she said finally. "Perhaps of a personal nature."

Elvis gazed up at Nancy Pollard. "I'm a friend of Freddy Littlejon's," he said quietly.

Pollard burst into laughter—louder and more raucously than Elvis could imagine anything that he said deserved. That over-the-top performance again; even Gene Nelson would have reigned that one in.

"I'll be damned," she said. "So for once Squirm was telling the truth."

Funny, those were pretty much the same words Warden Reardon had used.

"You broke his heart, you know," Elvis said, not taking his eyes off her.

"Well, he broke *mine*!" Pollard snapped back.

"By carrying on with that girl?"

"No!" Pollard howled. "By *killing* that girl!"

"And what makes you so sure he did that, Miss Pollard?"

"The same thing that makes everybody else so sure," Pollard said. "Absolutely everything. For godssake, the man has admitted to being a rapist. A rapist of underage girls."

"Who did he admit that to?"

"His friends," Pollard said.

"You mean Mr. Grieves."

"For one," Pollard said.

"For one and only, as far as I can tell," Elvis said. "And what makes you so sure that Grieves is telling the truth?"

Pollard turned, walked slowly back to her chair, and sat down again.

"Look, Mr. Presley," she said softly. "I cannot tell you how impressed I am with your loyalty to Squirm. It's not often that a man of your—your stature—takes an interest in someone like him. I mean, it's really quite touching. But I think your concern is misplaced. Squirm is a murderer and he only got what he deserved." For the first time since he'd limped into Pollard's office, Elvis heard what sounded like genuine sincerity in her voice.

"So what you said at the trial is all true," Elvis said gently. "About Squirm's, you know, his dress-up games with you at home."

Nancy Pollard's face blushed that shade of flaming crimson which is reserved for redheads.

"There ... There are all kinds of truth, Mr. Presley," she said. Elvis stared back at Nancy Pollard, struggling actress turned big-time MGM executive.

"Ma'am, I think you've been in the moving picture business too long. Way too long," he said. "There's only one kind of truth I know of—the *true* kind. Now did you play those dress-up games with Squirm or didn't you?"

Pollard's blush deepened several more degrees to an unhealthy-looking purple. This surely wasn't acting; maybe even her natural responses were over the top.

"We played those games," she whispered.

The moment Pollard said this, there was a peppy knock on the office door and Aronson's perky voice gurgled, "Ready for the surprise?"

"Yes, yes, ready, Maryjane," Pollard answered, her blush miraculously vanishing.

Aronson came sailing in with a tan cardboard box in her hands. She set it down with a flourish in the middle of the table. Elvis expected the worst—maybe a Hollywood chef's rendition of sweet potato pie. Aronson lifted off the box top and pulled out a pair of men's shoes—suede shoes of a luminous shade of blue. She set these on the table too.

"Do you know what this is?" Aronson trilled.

"Fifty thousand dollars!" Pollard chimed back in a heartbeat.

"All you have to do is wear them in your next picture," Aronson said. "Just wear them, nothing else. It doesn't matter what kind of story it is. And the Bonavita Shoe Company forks over fifty grand."

Elvis cupped a hand across his eyes. At that moment, he would have given just about anything to be back in Memphis, sitting at the counter of Floyd's Diner and drinking a cup of coffee with the boys.

"Product placement," Pollard said. "It's a gold mine."

"Like every time someone drinks a Coke in a picture—and you can see the label—the cash register rings," Aronson went on breathlessly. "But this is much bigger. Much. Fifty thousand is unheard of."

"Colonel Parker is all for it," Pollard said. "But, of course, he wanted us to run it by you first."

Elvis reached for his crutches and pulled himself up onto them. He started immediately for the door. Aronson raced after him, catching up with him as he swung into the hallway. She smiled prettily up at him.

"Let's stay in touch, Mr. Presley. I like your ideas very much," Aronson said softly. "I'm working on some projects of my own, and very soon I'm going to be in a position to do pictures Nancy couldn't dream of making."

Elvis gaped at Aronson quizzically and hobbled the heck out of there.

11
DELIVER ME FROM EVIL

THE sign on the door said ARCHIVES. The door was half open and had enough tobacco smoke wafting out of it to send an entire encyclopedia in smoke signals. Elvis poked at the door with the tip of a crutch and it swung open to reveal two men, one middle aged, bald, and wearing rimless glasses, the other in his twenties with too much hair. Both were puffing putrid-smelling cigars. They were sitting in the dark splicing film on a Moviola, and when they saw Elvis in the doorway, the young one gasped, *"Caramba!"* and the other, "Unbelievable!"

"This the movie library?" Elvis asked. A go-fer upstairs had directed him down to the second basement of the main MGM building.

Both men sprang to their feet and gaped at Elvis. It was the kind of reaction that Elvis was used to in public, but not here in the palace of stars. Probably not that many luminaries got this far underground.

"Library, archives. Right, Mr. Presley," the bald one sputtered.

"Anything we can do for you, sir?" asked the long-haired one.

"Hope so," Elvis said, leaning against the doorjamb to ease the strain under his arms. "I wanted to see clips of a particular actress."

"Not a problem," the older man said.

"Would you like to sit down, Mr. Presley?" the younger one said, gesturing to the seat he had just vacated.

"Thank you," Elvis said. He hobbled around the Moviola and sat down heavily.

"May I just say one thing?" the younger man asked excitedly. His partner frowned disapprovingly.

"Go ahead," Elvis said.

"I just have to say that you were fabulous in *Jailhouse Rock*. So sensitive. So vulnerable. We watch it all the time down here."

"That's kind of you to say," Elvis said.

"I mean it sincerely," the man went on excitedly. "As an actor, I put you right up there with James Dean and Marlon Brando."

Elvis studied his face for hints of toadyism or sarcasm, but the man actually seemed to mean what he was saying.

"How about Richard Burton or Peter O'Toole?" The question popped out of Elvis's mouth before he could think the better of it.

"Are you kidding?" the young man replied emphatically. "Those two are actor's actors, not *real* actors. Every little thing they do is so deliberate, like they always want you to see all the technique and effort they're putting in it. Really, you can't see the characters for the acting."

"Absolutely true," his partner echoed. "Neither of them can touch you or Dean."

Elvis felt embarrassed by how much pleasure he took from the pair's professional analysis.

"The name of the actress I want to see is McDougal, Holly McDougal," Elvis said. "She was just a bit player."

The two men looked at one another warily.

"She was murdered, you know," the young one said.

"So I understand," Elvis replied. "Can you help me out?"

"Of course, Mr. Presley."

The older man flipped on the overhead florescent lights. The room was far larger than Elvis had thought. In fact, it was cavernous, nut and bolt metal shelves going off in every direction almost as far as the eye could see, every one of them loaded with film reels. The two men raced off in opposite directions, cigar smoke trailing behind them. Less than five minutes later, they returned with a total of five reels. Four were B pictures, three of them musicals, one a circus picture. The fifth was an uncovered reel with less than a one-inch depth of film on it. The label read MCDOUGAL, HOLLY—SCREEN TEST. Elvis reached for it.

"Want me to see what screening rooms are available?" the younger man asked.

Elvis hesitated.

"Or we could thread it up right here," the older man said, gesturing toward the Moviola.

"Let's do it that way," Elvis said.

The pair set to work immediately, removing the film they had been splicing—apparently they had been repairing a brittle old master—and threading in McDougal's screen test. When they had finished, they remained standing on either side of Elvis. The opaque glass monitor on the Moviola was only a three-inch square. Elvis crouched over it. "Let's go," he said.

First, a slate: MCDOUGAL, HOLLY, SCREEN TEST. 9.12.59. TAKE: #1. And then there she was, a wavy-haired blonde with blue saucer eyes and a turned-up nose wearing a pleated white blouse, short plaid kilt, ankle socks, and patent-leather Mary Janes. She was sitting on a high stool in front of a pale blue backdrop, and she was giggling. An off-screen male voice said, "We're rolling," and Holly straightened up, smoothed her blouse, and looked excitedly into the camera.

"Hi," she said. "My name is Holly McDougal and I am eighteen years old and I have just always, *always*, wanted to be an actress."

She paused, looking expectantly off to one side. "Your audition piece," the off-screen voice said.

"Can I get off the stool?" Holly asked.

"Sure," replied the off-screen voice.

Holly slipped off the stool, turned her back to the camera, then faced it again with her eyebrows now puckered and her mouth slightly open, her lower lip dangling. Or was it quivering? Abruptly, she began darting about, waving her hands around wildly. Swatting flies? Playing tennis? Whatever it was, Miss McDougal was clearly *acting*.

"'These are love letters, yellowing with antiquity, all from one boy,'" she recited. "'Give them back to me! . . . The touch of your hand insults them. . . . Now that you've touched them I'll burn them. . . . Poems a dead boy wrote.'"

On either side of Elvis, the two archivists tittered.

"God help us, it's *Streetcar*," the older one said.

"A *Streetcar Named Perspire*," the other said archly.

Holly McDougal got to the line, "'I'm not young and vulnerable any more,'" when the off-screen voice interrupted with, "Thank you, Miss McDougal. That should be enough."

The girl froze. She looked crestfallen. Her eyes started to tear up.

"Do you dance, Holly?" another off-screen male voice asked. This voice was cheery and sounded vaguely familiar.

"Oh, yes!" the girl answered brightly. "I've taken ballet for five years. Tap for three."

Some muffled off-screen discussion, the screen went blank for a moment, then another slate appeared: MCDOUGAL, HOLLY, SCREEN TEST. 9.12.59. TAKE: #2. The stool had been removed and Holly stood expectantly in front of the camera, her hands on her hips. Suddenly, the music blasted on: Elvis's 1956 recording of "Blue Suede Shoes." Holly McDougal began to dance.

No awkward fly swatting this time. Instantly, the young woman was rocking and rolling with abandon, her slender arms swinging, her head bobbing. Now she was spinning, kicking her bare legs to the height of her shoulders, her kilt rising, then twirling up to her waist exposing red-satin panties. And then her hips began to go, at first in a kind of parody of Elvis's own moves, rhythmic staccato shifts from left to right on the offbeat, a visual syncopation with a sly twist. But then Holly's hips went off on their own, grinding slowly in a wide arc, the rhythm gradually picking up as the music rose in volume, now gyrating faster and faster, the kilt fluttering up and down over flashes of red satin. At some point, the top button of the girl's blouse had come undone; at another, the second and the third. As she gyrated, the blouse flapped open and closed over her high, shapely breasts. Apparently, Holly McDougal was not wearing anything under her prim schoolgirl blouse.

Throughout the performance, the second off-screen voice could be heard urging Holly on with, "That's it, baby!" and "Show us what you've got!" and "You're killing me, sweetheart!" When the music ended, the girl twirled to a stop, then sashayed with an insolent smile right up to the camera and planted a wet kiss on the lens. The screen went blank again.

"Deliver me from evil," the middle-aged man said, hitting the stop button on the Moviola.

"Turns out she was only seventeen when they shot that," the younger man said.

"Not even," the other one murmured. "Still a few months shy of seventeen."

Elvis sat perfectly still, staring at the blank monitor, a sick feeling in his gut. The fire in his groin from watching Holly's little exhibition was still there, still tingling, and it revolted him. Everything about it revolted him. That she was only a child. That the body which had just now tantalized him was long gone, dead and gone at the hands of a grotesque killer. And, on top of that, hearing his own voice as the soundtrack for Holly McDougal's precociously torrid rock and roll fandango made the whole thing

even more repulsive. *Elvis, the Pelvis*, corrupter of youthful innocence. He felt like begging God for forgiveness.

"That Wayne, he sure knows how to get them going, doesn't
he?" the younger man was saying.

"Wayne?"

"You know, Wayne LeFevre," the young man said to Elvis.
"They like to bring him in for the screen tests of those young girls.
He has a special knack for bringing out the sauciness in them."

So that's who that familiar voice belonged to—Wayne LeFevre,
Elvis's double, the man who offered himself up as a consolation
prize every time Elvis spurned the advances of some ardent chorus
girl. Somehow it fit that Wayne would be the in-house cheerleader
who brought out the sauciness in eager young auditioners. And
after the screen test, what? Did Wayne parlay his helpful hints
into some personal action? Had he taken Holly McDougal off to
an empty office and made his moves on the child? Elvis's disgust
redoubled.

"Looks like there's more on there," the younger archivist was
saying, gesturing to the reel on the Moviola. "Want to see it?"

Elvis sighed. "I guess so," he said.

On TAKE #3, Holly was joined by two other women, one on
either side of her, all three in black leotards. This time the music
was a Broadway show tune; apparently, they had taught Holly
the steps before the take. Obviously, the purpose was to see how
she worked with other dancers, how well she fit in. The routine
was low-level Vegas—high kicks with their hands on each other's
shoulders, a pinwheel thing with Holly in the center, then some
snaky shimmying. Holly excelled at the shimmying—it began at
her knees, worked its way up to her hips, and then her entire torso
did a shake, rattle, and roll that had her fine breasts undulating
under the leotard like conical Jell-o molds. It was surely more
than a healthy man could bear.

Elvis noticed that the dancer on Holly's right kept stealing
glances at Holly while they shimmied. This girl, also a blonde,
was taller and thinner and obviously more practiced, but her own
undulations could not begin to compete with the bouncy sensu-
ality of Holly's, and it was clear from the expression on her face

that she knew it. Knew it and resented it. It was like Gene Nelson said, two things the camera always catches are boredom and envy. Well, even on this three-by-three screen, the envy screamed out at Elvis. But who the heck was that screaming it?

"Freeze it, can you?" he suddenly said.

The image froze and Elvis leaned in closer to the little monitor. By God, he was right: the envious blond dancer was Nancy Pollard. Apparently, as Nannette Poulette, she had been a blonde, but the face was the same. And so was the small-breasted, willowy body. How about that? Poulette/Pollard had been jealous of Holly McDougal's shimmy long before she began practicing it on the stunt-shack cot with her boyfriend, Squirm.

A minute later, the film flapped off the reel; the screen test was over. Elvis's two hosts asked him to autograph stills from *Jailhouse Rock*, which he gladly did, finally learning their names: Paddy Spence and Paddy Spence, Jr., father and son. Archiving film was the family trade.

Elvis hobbled back down the basement hallway to the elevator and rang for it. When the door slid open, there was Colonel Parker standing inside, gazing out at him. Once again, Parker had that look of a scolding father on his face. If Elvis hadn't been on crutches, he would have bolted.

"Heard you were down here, son," the Colonel drawled. "Now this kind of thing can't be doing your ankle much good, can it?"

Elvis stepped into the elevator without responding. He had intended to go up to the ground floor to meet Joey, but instead he punched the button for the floor below it, the first basement. He didn't want to spend a minute longer than necessary with Parker today.

"So how'd your meeting with Nancy Pollard go?" Parker asked. There was enough syrup in his voice for a double-dip sundae.

"It went," Elvis answered. There was no sense in even asking how the Colonel knew about the meeting.

"She doesn't have any real power, you know," Parker said. "Girl couldn't green-light a two-minute cartoon."

"That a fact?" Elvis said. "Then how come her title's director of project development?"

"Politics," Parker responded, simpering. "It's all politics in this business. Who you know and who you're sleeping with."

The elevator shuddered to a stop and the door slid open.

"So who are you sleeping with, Colonel?" Elvis asked, deadpan.

Parker cracked up like it was the funniest darned thing he'd ever heard. "Mrs. Parker on alternate Tuesdays," he replied. "It's all the politics she can stand."

Elvis stepped off the elevator, but Parker held the door open. He reached into his shirt pocket and withdrew a slip of paper. "My girl took a call for you from that . . . friend of yours in Alamo," he said, handing the paper to Elvis. "This something I should know about?"

"No," Elvis said. "But there is something I did want to talk to you about."

"What's that, son?"

"Those blue suede shoes you want me to wear in my next picture for fifty grand," Elvis said.

Parker beamed. "Incredible deal, isn't it?"

"I'd sooner go barefoot," Elvis said.

12
THE BUM

THE message from Billy was short and simple: a telephone number with an Atlanta exchange and "Call after seven P.M." It looked like Billy had located Connie Spinelli already, God love him. Elvis tucked the note in his pocket.

Elvis found the stairwell and limped up to the first floor with both crutches under his right shoulder and his left hand on the railing. His ankle was throbbing like the devil again, so at the landing, he took out the vial of painkillers and bit off half a pill. Just enough to dull the pain without losing his mental edge.

The first thing Elvis saw when he pushed open the stairwell door was Joey and the Colonel standing next to a potted palm in the vestibule. Colonel was in full-command mode, wagging a stubby finger in Joey's face and jawing a mile a minute. No doubt giving Joey instructions to get Elvis home and in bed ASAP: time is money and sprained ankles are untimely.

Elvis let the door swing closed in front of him, still standing in the stairwell. He dragged himself back down the stairs, then followed the first basement corridor to the rear of the building and limped back up to the first floor. No sign of Joey or the Colonel from here—they were on the other side of the elevator shaft. Elvis slipped out a back door and motioned to an MGM valet who was standing under an awning drinking Coke out a bottle. Nice product placement. Elvis asked the kid to bring his car around. The boy hesitated, eyeing Elvis's bandaged left ankle.

"Not a problem," Elvis said, winking. "It's my brake foot."

It wasn't a problem, either. The Eldorado had automatic shift with plenty of room to stretch out his leg where the clutch would have been. He probably should have driven himself to the studio in the first place, except that Joanie and Joey would have kicked up a fuss. For a motherless child, he sure had a truckload of mothers.

Elvis headed out to the edge of the parking lot, then swung around onto the driveway, skirting the main entrance of the MGM building. He slowed to a halt at the front gate and rolled down his window. Nobody in the guard house to lift the gate. Elvis waited a couple of minutes, then tapped out "Shave and a Haircut" on his horn. A few seconds later, the guard came chugging up behind the car.

"Sorry, Mr. Presley," he said. "Had to take care of the flag."

He stepped into the guard house and the gate swung up. Just as Elvis started through, he caught a glimpse of the studio flagpole in his side mirror: it was at half-mast. Elvis inched back to the guard house.

"Somebody die?" he asked the guard, gesturing toward the pole.

"Nobody important," the guard said. "But they want me to lower it for anyone connected to MGM. Turns out that's half of L.A."

Elvis nodded. "Who was it?"

"Stuntman," the guard said. "But not on the lot—nothing to do with a picture. Accident at a rodeo somewhere in Nevada. Got kicked in the head by a crazy bull. Dumb way to die, wouldn't you say, Mr. Presley?"

Elvis felt his heart accelerate. "What was his name?"

The guard lifted a clipboard off of a hook and looked at it. "Cathcart," he read. "Will Cathcart."

Elvis's head began to spin. He closed his eyes. For a moment, he felt like he was again suspended from that stunt harness, a puppet swinging uncontrollably, colliding with struts and walls, raucous laughter soaring up at him. *Mickey Grieves's laughter.*

Elvis opened his eyes and hit the accelerator. He pulled out on the access road and headed for the freeway. Cathcart had written that he had important things to tell Elvis right after he got back from the rodeo. God in heaven, you didn't need to read Dr. Sigmund Freud to know that Will Cathcart's death was no accident, whether it involved some crazy bull or not.

Elvis was on the freeway before he realized that he was instinctively heading for West Hollywood—Clifford's office. The day before yesterday, Squirm Littlejon's case may have been a diversion from all the little messes in Elvis's life, but that day was long ago and far away. A young man was dead. Elvis had been threatened within an inch of his life. If Holly McDougal's mother thought her daughter was a choir girl, she'd been sitting in the wrong pew. And Nancy Pollard was either a better liar than she was an actress, or Squirm Littlejon was hiding something.

Elvis pulled into the left lane to pass a poky Good Humor truck. And that is when, in his rearview mirror, he saw the blue Beetle slip in behind him. The same one as this morning, no doubt about it. The same bearded driver with a nightwatch cap pulled down to his eyebrows, and this time the driver was waving something in his right hand. It looked too large to be a gun, but Elvis wasn't about to hang around to see what it was. He pushed down on the accelerator and shot ahead about thirty yards until he was a car length behind a station wagon loaded with children in party hats. Elvis swung into the right lane, flooring it.

Man, he was flying now. Weaving in and out of all three lanes. He punched on the radio and like magic, there was Hank Snow filling the air with "It Don't Hurt Anymore." No, Hank, it don't hurt. Not just now. Don't know why, but the hurt is gone. Or maybe it's still there but it don't matter. Elvis began to sing along with

Snow, substituting "It don't matter any more" for "I don't hurt any more." He glanced in his rearview mirror. No blue Beetle. "No blue Beetle any more," he crooned, lurching back into the left lane and sailing ahead like a human cannonball.

The chorus came on, but this time old Hank had added some winds, a flutey thing that wound around the melody like a silver ribbon. He'd added some lights too, red and blue strobes that bounced around the interior of the Eldorado on the offbeat. Man, how did Old Hank do that? The man was a genius.

"Pull over! Pull over immediately!"

Elvis looked again in his rearview mirror. That's where the lights were coming from. And that flutey thing too.

"Pull into the right lane now!"

Elvis pulled across two lanes in one swoop, then coasted to a stop on the shoulder, the cop car just behind him. He rolled down his window. Great air out there. *Fabulous* air out there.

"You're a menace, buddy! Doing ninety-plus," the policeman barked. "License and registration." He was a big man, no hat, no hair, and a fancy pair of aviator sunglasses. His face hovered in the car window like a shark in a fish tank.

Elvis handed him his license.

"Holy Mother of God, Elvis Presley!" the shark exclaimed.

"Yes, sir," Elvis said. "Sorry I was speeding. But somebody was following me and I was trying to shake him."

"I didn't recognize you, Mr. Presley," the policeman said. "I mean, I must stop one kid a day who dresses up like you. Sideburns, hair, the whole deal."

"No problem," Elvis said. "Like I said, it's this man in a blue Beetle. Been on my tail all day."

"Probably wants your autograph."

"I think he wants more than that, Officer," Elvis said.

"Well, *I* sure as hell want your autograph," the policeman said, handing Elvis a traffic citation. "If you don't mind, make it out to Tom—Tom Schultz."

"On this?"

"If that's all right, Mr. Presley."

Elvis inscribed the traffic ticket and returned it to Officer Schultz.

"Thank you," Schultz said. He removed his sunglasses and looked intently into Elvis's face. "Excuse me if I'm out of line, Mr. Presley, but are you feeling all right?"

"Just fine, thank you," Elvis said.

"Good. I'm glad to hear that," Schultz said.

"Why shouldn't I be, Officer?"

"Just something about your eyes," Schultz said. "Look a little glassy. Sort of wobbly too. Like maybe you're coming down with something."

Elvis laughed. "Oh, I've just been singing, Officer. Singing my fool head off with Hank Snow here, and it's enough to bring tears to my eyes."

Elvis turned up the radio by way of demonstration, but Hank was now gone, replaced by Jimmy Gilmour and the Fireballs singing "Sugar Shack." Not much of number, that one. Elvis snapped it off.

"Well, you take care of yourself, Mr. Presley," the police-man was saying. "And if you ever need anything—escort, special detail—you just give me a ring, okay?" Schultz handed Elvis his card, winking. "Tell you what, Elvis, I'll escort you a bit now. Make sure no beetles are on your tail, especially none of those new English Beetles—Ringo, Paul, none of 'em. Ha!"

With this, the officer of the law burst into a boyish giggle and sauntered back to his car. He followed Elvis, his lights flashing, all the way to the West Hollywood exit.

Elvis had to smile when he saw the note on Clifford's door: INVESTIGATION IN PROGRESS, BACK BY FIVE. The man had flair. Of course, there was something of the little kid who was just *playing* at a grown-up job in the way he put it—"Investigation in progress." Sounded like something Tubby might say to Little Lulu. Then again, the same could be said about Elvis himself, that he was just *playing* at being a detective. Surely that is the way the Colonel would put it.

Elvis darn well didn't feel like limping down the stairs again and waiting for Clifford in his car, but there were no chairs in the hallway. He could knock on the chiropractor's door—DR. HIRAM GOLDSTEIN, DC, SERVING THE WELL ADJUSTED SINCE 1946—or on the door to the Spanish travel agency, but just now he wasn't up to being recognized and all that usually followed from that.

He limped on one crutch over to the corner between Clifford's office and the travel agency, set both crutches against the wall, lowered himself onto the floor, and leaned back with his legs stretched out in front of him. That felt a whole lot better. Man, he was tired. He let his head loll against the wall, his eyelids fluttering. He was about to let his eyes close completely, when he suddenly saw another man sprawled on the floor across the hallway from him. The guy looked like a derelict who had crawled inside to catch a snooze away from the street. His face was blank, his eyes rheumy, his mouth slack. A bum.

It only lasted an instant. Then Elvis realized that he was looking at himself reflected in the frameless mirror next to Dr. Goldstein's door. *He* was that guy with the glassy eyes slumped against the wall next to a pair of crutches. *He* was the bum who had crawled inside like a wounded dog. Elvis put a hand to his face, watched his reflection mime him. *His twin*. The man he would have been. Could have been. Still could be. His eyelids began fluttering again, then closed completely, and Elvis drifted off into the sleep of the wordless song.

13
EL VEZ PEREZ-LEE

"YOU look like crap."

"What?"

"*You*, pal. You look terrible."

Elvis blinked open his eyes. Regis Clifford was stooped over him, waving a paper cup of coffee under his nose. Elvis looked around; he was in Clifford's office, slouched in the chair across from the attorney's desk.

"How'd I get in here?"

"Doc Goldstein helped. In fact, he gave you a little adjustment along the way. Your neck crackled like a string of firecrackers."

Clifford handed the cup to Elvis who took a long swallow. It tasted awful, but did the trick. Coming fully awake, Elvis realized that he had enjoyed another one of those deep and renewing mini slumbers.

"Ready to hear my report?" Clifford said spiritedly. He looked peppier and more clear eyed than either of the other times Elvis had seen him. *Far* peppier.

"I'm ready," Elvis said, taking another gulp of bitter coffee.

"Okay," Regis said, sitting on the corner of his desk. "First, we're going to Mexico tomorrow. Leave at five in the morning on the Tequila Express. Hector—Dr. Garcia—is expecting us. And listen to this, he has new data for us, something he's done on his own. Didn't want to tell me what it was until we got there, but he says it proves that Littlejon is innocent." Regis leaned toward Elvis. "You do have a passport, I hope."

"I think so. From the army." Elvis shrugged. "But I left it in Memphis."

"Okay, okay. I'll come up with something. But now for the big enchilada." Regis rubbed his palms together. "Norma McDougal, Holly's big sister. Norma and I had a lovely little lunch today at The Palms in Santa Monica. Crab salad, avocados, Chardonnay. Courtesy of my employer, by the way, but it was well worth it, believe me, Elvis."

"I'm sure it was."

"She wasn't hard to find, actually," Regis said. "Still lives in the same neighborhood, although not with her mother any more. She works in a nursing home. A lot of bedpan duty, from what I gather. Let's just say she dreams of better things to come."

Regis paused, his eyes flicking around the office, clearly scanning for a little evening pick-me-up. But apparently he was too eager to continue with his story to interrupt himself.

"Anyway, I didn't pull any punches with her," he went on. "I told her we were reopening the Littlejon case. Didn't mention your name, of course. And I asked her what she knew about her late little sister's love life."

"And?"

"Nothing," Regis replied, with an odd smile. "She didn't know a damned thing about it."

Elvis screwed up his face. "Where's the enchilada, Regis?"

"The enchilada is that Norma was just thrilled to finally be talking with a bona-fide lawyer. That's me. Because Norma needed some expert legal advice on how to get her hands on Holly's savings account, not to mention her safety deposit box. It seems that Holly was a good saver. *Very* good. She left behind two hundred and fifty thousand dollars. And God knows what in her safety deposit box."

"That's a lot of savings for a chorus girl," Elvis said.

"I know you people are notoriously overpaid, but I'd say so," Regis said.

"Where do you suppose she got it?"

"I don't know and neither does Norma," Regis said. "To put it mildly, I don't think the sisters were very close. I've seen pictures of Holly, and the gene pool seems to have overspent on her. Making up for the fact that it underspent on Norma. She's more than a bit chunky and somehow her eyes don't match. And if she ever forgot for a minute that she wasn't the family beauty, apparently Holly was always ready to remind her."

"Doesn't Holly's money belong to the mother?" Elvis asked.

"Technically, if there was no will, yes," Regis said. "But Mrs. McDougal doesn't know about the savings account. Or the safety deposit box, for that matter. Anyway, it's kind of open ended until we find out where exactly the money came from. There's always the chance that it was ill-got gains."

"How does Norma know about it anyhow?"

"She found the bank book and the key cleaning out Holly's room," Regis said. "This was only a few months ago. Mrs. McDougal wouldn't let anybody touch the room for years after

Holly's death. Kept it as kind of a shrine, like Miss Haversham's wedding house."

"Miss Haversham?"

"Dickens. *Great Expectations*. You should read it, Elvis."

"I'll get to it after Dr. Freud," Elvis said. "So where do we go with this, Regis?"

"Well, it certainly might be helpful to get into that safety deposit box," Regis said. "The stuff people put in those boxes usually come with a story attached. Something you can trace back to where it came from. A lot more promising than anonymous bank notes."

"And how exactly do we get into the safety deposit box?"

"I don't know, but I'm thinking about it. That's what I like about this business—the challenge."

"Right, the challenge," Elvis said. His stomach grumbled. Little wonder, he hadn't had a bite since his breakfast toast. He looked at his watch—7:10. "Hold on—I got to make a phone call, Regis. Right now."

"Go ahead," Regis said. "I've got business to attend to anyhow."

He sauntered out of the office like a man on a mission, that mission undoubtedly being a trip to the corner liquor store.

Elvis retrieved the scrap of paper Colonel had given him and dialed the long-distance operator. He gave her the Atlanta phone number. It rang just once, then, "Hello. Who is this?"

"Elvis Presley, ma'am."

"What's the password?" the woman said.

"Password?"

"Yes, you're supposed to have a password so I know it's really you."

It seems Parker's secretary hadn't bothered to jot down that part.

"I'm sorry, Miss Spinelli, but nobody gave me a password," Elvis said.

"I can't risk it then," Spinelli said. "Good-bye, Mr. Presley, or whoever you are."

"Wait a second," Elvis said. "Billy Jackson gave you this password, right?"

"That's right. He's a good man, by the way. And quite attractive."

Elvis had to smile at that. Billy would be happy to hear that he still had the old charm. "You have good taste," he said to Connie Spinelli.

"He took me out for drinks to a black bar," she went on. "I've always wanted to go in one of those, but it's not something a woman does on her own. Not a white woman, at least."

"I imagine not," Elvis said. It was beginning to sound as if old Billy had made the most of this personal favor.

"Well, I'm sorry we can't talk more," Spinelli was saying. "They have a way of tracking you down and making your life miserable, you know."

"*Who* does?"

"I'm sorry," Spinelli said. "I can't do this."

"*Selma!*" Elvis blurted out spontaneously. "The password is 'Selma.'"

"Well, why didn't you say that in the first place, Mr. Presley?" Spinelli exclaimed.

"I don't know, Miss Spinelli," Elvis said. "So, what can you tell me about Holly McDougal?"

"A lot," Spinelli said. Then, "Listen, you're not calling from the studio are you? They can—"

"No, I'm at a friend's phone," Elvis said. "And there's nobody else here at the moment."

"Okay, thanks," Spinelli said. She took an audible deep breath before continuing. "I know you're not supposed to speak ill of the dead. But the truth is the truth, living or dead, right Mr. Presley?"

"That's right."

"Well, Holly was not a bad kid. Not really. But she had the bug, the same bug most of the girls in the business have, but maybe a little more so. She wanted to make it big, big as it gets. She wanted to be a star. Like you, Mr. Presley."

"I see," Elvis said, although the way Spinelli put it, being a star didn't sound like something that any healthy person would aspire to. Maybe she was right.

"You can't say that Holly's approach was particularly original," Spinelli went on. "All those gags about the casting director's couch didn't come out of thin air, you know. I'd say more than half of the starlets and chorus girls put in time on somebody's couch. Hell, Marilyn Monroe, may her soul rest in peace, wasn't averse to keeping the big bosses happy in a personal way. Comes with the territory, I guess."

"I guess it does," Elvis said. None of this was really a surprise to him, but it gave him a queasy feeling anyhow.

"But with Holly, the whole thing kind of took on a life of its own," Spinelli went on. "I don't know exactly where you draw the line between trading favors for parts in movies and being an out-and-out call girl, but I'd say that Holly crossed that line wherever it is."

"She told you this?"

"Certainly did," Spinelli said. "I'd be doing her nails—that's my specialty, you know—I'd be doing her nails and she would chatter away about this one and that one she'd been with. I've got to say, the whole business didn't seem like a chore to her. She seemed to take real pride in it. Nothing wrong with that, I suppose—taking pride in your work."

"Did she mention any of the men by name?" Elvis asked.

"Some," Spinelli said. "A couple of casting directors I knew of. A few talent agents. And a whole lot of other people I never heard of. I didn't keep track. It's quite a list."

"So she was, you know—she was charging a fee for her services?" Elvis asked.

Spinelli laughed. "Why, Mr. Presley, that's hard for you to ask, isn't it? You *are* a Southern gentleman, just like they say. I'm still not used to that out here. Not after Hollywood."

"She was just so young, that's all," Elvis said, feeling embarrassed, although he was not sure why.

"Holly was seventeen going on thirty, like most of them," Spinelli said. "Girls grow up faster out there. Age faster too. Believe me, that's something you learn very quickly in the makeup department."

Elvis scratched his jaw. He did not have any idea what a call girl charged, but it was hard to imagine it adding up to a quarter of a million dollars in just a couple of years.

"Where . . . Where did Holly meet her . . . clients?" he asked.

Spinelli laughed again. "Oh, this is the real crazy part," she said. "Holly set herself up right there on the lot. She said that way she was always available if a part came up. She'd check in all day with the line producers—you know, to see if some chorus girl called in sick or broke her ankle or something. And if a part came up, she'd just leave some guy stranded, waiting for her in the stunt shack."

"The stunt shack? Is that where she—"

"Yes, that was Holly's little base of operations," Spinelli said. "It didn't strike me as a Paris boudoir exactly. Not particularly private, for one thing. Have you ever been out there?"

"Just yesterday," Elvis said. No need to tell Spinelli about his harness adventure.

"So you know what I mean," Spinelli went on. "But Holly said that most of the men liked it. Something macho about the setting. You'll have to excuse me, Mr. Presley, but when it comes to men's sexual predilections, I get out of my depth pretty fast. That's probably why I'm still single."

"To tell you the truth, Miss Spinelli, I don't understand that much about it myself," Elvis said.

This time Spinelli laughed so hard that she had to set down the receiver for a moment. When she came back on, she said, "I'm sorry, Mr. Presley, but that sure takes the prize—*Elvis Presley* doesn't understand that much about sex—"

"I just meant the strange stuff, ma'am," Elvis interjected quickly and a little more loudly than he had intended.

"Well, God bless you for that, Mr. Presley," Spinelli said. "It takes a real man to admit something like that."

Elvis was about to thank her for the compliment, but stopped himself, realizing that he wanted to get off this little side topic as swiftly as possible.

"So all the stuntmen must have known what was going on," he said.

"I don't know about *all* of them," Spinelli said. "Some of those stunt kids can be pretty wet behind the ears. The cowboys and rodeo punks especially. But the regulars knew what was up, all right. They took out her rent in trade, if you know what I mean."

"I know what you mean," Elvis said. He looked up; Regis was sailing back in the office door with a smug expression on his face. "One more thing, Miss Spinelli. A few years back, you made a date with an attorney, man named Regis Clifford, to talk about Holly. But you never made it. In fact, you more or less disappeared after that. What happened?"

For almost a minute, Connie Spinelli did not say a word.

"Ma'am?"

"I was told to leave," Spinelli said flatly.

"Who told you?"

"I didn't see his face," Spinelli said. "He had a gas mask on and an army uniform. First World War. Actually, it looked kind of new, like it was straight out of MGM wardrobe. But his gun wasn't hard to see."

"I'm sorry you had to go through that, Miss Spinelli," Elvis said.

"It's all right," she answered. "I'm actually much happier out here."

"We'll be in touch, ma'am. You take good care of yourself."

"Mr. Presley?"

"Yes?"

"Do you mind if I ask you something personal?"

Elvis put his hand to his forehead. He surely did not want to discuss the peculiarities of male sexuality with Connie Spinelli any more, but God knows, he owed her.

"What is it?" Elvis said.

"Is your friend, Dr. Jackson, married?" she asked, sounding just about seventeen—a *Tennessee* seventeen.

"No, ma'am," Elvis answered, smiling. "Not the last time I heard, at least."

The moment Elvis hung up, Regis presented him with a little blue booklet. It was a United States passport.

"Freshly minted," Regis said proudly. "My pal Rodriguez at the travel agency just happened to have a blank on hand. We clipped a photo of you out of *Silver Screen* magazine and laminated it in. Looks perfect. The funny thing is, Rodriguez never heard of you and when he typed in your name, he spelled it, 'El Vez Perez-Lee.' Cuban Chinese. It's a good thing I caught it."

Elvis opened up the passport. The photograph of him was a still from the pre-release publicity kit for *Viva Las Vegas*. You could see where Senor Rodriguez had scissored Ann-Margret out of the frame.

"I underestimate you, Regis," Elvis said, smiling. "I was sure you'd gone out for a drink."

"You don't underestimate me, Elvis," Regis replied. "Rodriguez and I toasted our good work with a shot of tequila."

14
HOT SAUCE

ELVIS brought Regis up to date between forkfuls of *barbacoa de lomo* at La Cucina, a tiny Mexican cafe on the same block as Regis's office. The Mexican barbecue was so hot you could feel it burning all the way down to your gut, but God knows, it was the real thing for a change, even if you did have to excavate it from some kind of moldy leaf to get at it. Elvis told Regis about Cathcart's death; his meeting with Nancy Pollard, and her insistence that she had been telling the truth on the witness stand; the man in the blue Beetle who had been following him; and finally about Holly McDougal's extracurricular activities as described by Connie Spinelli. Regis, who had only ordered a bowl of rice and a pitcher of sangria, grew increasingly excited with each piece of news.

"My friend, it's a puzzle wrapped in an enigma," Clifford said. "But we are on our way. Yes, indeed, the hounds have picked up the scent."

Elvis sawed off a piece of fried plantain and stuck it in his mouth to cool down his palate.

"I'll tell you, I can taste it already," Regis went on rhapsodically. "We petition the court, get a new trial, Littlejon's exonerated. It's all over the papers. And old LeRoy has got egg all over his face."

"Is that what this is all about for you, Regis?" Elvis asked. "Beating out your brother?"

Regis poured himself another glass of sangria and gulped it down before answering.

"I'd be lying if I said it wasn't a big chunk of it, Elvis," Regis said. "I'm not saying it's pretty. But revenge is what makes the world go around. Basic human emotion. Did you ever read *The Count of Monte Cristo*?"

"Even if it's your own kin?" Elvis asked. "Your own twin brother?"

"*Especially* if it's your twin brother," Regis answered. "How about a song about that, my friend? 'The Twin's Revenge.'" Regis winked, then called to the waiter in Spanish and in a flash another pitcher of sangria appeared. It was obvious that Regis was a regular at La Cucina; everybody called him, "Senor el Abogato," which, he explained, meant "Mr. Lawyer." But, for a nice change, nobody made a fuss about Elvis being there, nobody crowded him. Elvis had wondered if anyone even recognized him in the densely packed cafe—seeing as they were all immigrants—but now, in heavily accented English, the waiter asked, "Can I get you something, Senor Presley?"

"No, I'm just about full up, thank you," Elvis replied.

"My pleasure, Senor Presley."

Regis poured himself another glass of sangria. "There are three puzzles we need to unravel as soon as we get back from Mexico," he said. "First, how Holly accumulated that small fortune. I find it hard to believe myself that it's just profits from services rendered. Second, I'd like get a first-hand account of how your rodeo friend bit the proverbial dust. Probably it was just a coincidence—an accident at an inopportune time."

"I thought you said there were no accidents," Elvis said.

"I don't imagine Freud's theory applies to mad bulls," Regis said, winking. "And the third thing is, from what you say, I'm starting to wonder if our friend Squirm was telling us the whole truth, and nothing but the truth, about his sex life with Miss Pollard."

"Why don't we just go up to Tehachapi and ask him?" Elvis said.

"It's worth a try."

"I mean right now," Elvis said, mopping his mouth with a paper napkin.

"For chrissake, it's seven o'clock," Regis said. "I think it can wait. Squirm's not going anywhere."

"Neither am I," Elvis said. "My car's just outside."

"Jesus, Elvis, we have to get up at three in the morning to catch our plane," Regis pleaded.

"Best not sleep at all then."

"Listen, my friend, visiting hours ended four hours ago."

"I think I can get them to make an exception," Elvis said. "Do they have a pay phone in here?"

"No, they don't," Regis said emphatically.

"You can use our phone, Senor Presley." It was their waiter, as he removed Elvis's plate. "At the bar."

Regis rolled his eyes.

The bartender set the phone on the bar as Elvis approached. Next to it, he placed a shot glass of brandy. "Compliments of the house, Senor Presley," the bartender said. "I enjoy very much 'Rubias, Morenas Y Pelirrojas.'"

"Much obliged," Elvis said. He wanted to ask him what, exactly, that 'Rubias' thing meant, but it would have to wait. The operator put him right through to Warden Reardon's private line.

"Evening, Warden, it's me again, Elvis."

"Well, *hello*, Elvis," Reardon said. "I thought I'd be hearing from you pretty quick. It's perfect, isn't it?"

"Beg pardon?"

"*The Singing Warden.* Just what you're looking for, right? *Jailhouse Rock* with a new twist."

Only then did Elvis realize what the heck Reardon was talking about.

"Yes, sir, it's a real original," Elvis said. "Of course, I'll have to show it to a few folks before we can get started on it."

"Hey, that's show business," Reardon chirped. "But I've got a feeling you and I are going to be seeing a whole lot of each other."

"You bet," Elvis said. "How about tonight?" He told Reardon that he needed another few minutes with Fredrick Littlejon. It was, of course, no problem at all for the Singing Warden.

As he got into his car, Elvis's ankle began to throb again, throb and burn like crazy, as if the jalapenos in the barbecue sauce had coasted down his leg and taken up a command post in his foot. He reached into his jacket pocket for his pills.

"There is no way I am going to ride in this car if you take one of those," Regis blurted out, next to him.

"Just a half," Elvis said. "I drove over here on a half and I was clear as a whistle."

"That's what they all say, Elvis," Regis said.

"You drive then!" Elvis snapped.

"Wish I could. But I was relieved of my driving privileges a few years back. Drunk driving." Regis laughed. "You and I are quite a pair, aren't we?"

"I don't know what you're talking about," Elvis said irritably.

"I'm sure you don't," Regis said softly. "But just do me a favor, will you? No pill, not now. Please."

Elvis stuffed the bottle back into his pocket. Damn, for a fella with the health habits of a sewer rat, Regis sure was a prickly son of a gun about his driving conditions. Neither of them said another word until Elvis turned on to Route 14.

"Regis, there's something I been meaning to ask you about," Elvis said finally.

"Shoot," Regis said.

"It's this Dr. Freud you were talking about. He's got theories about sex, doesn't he?"

"A whole shelf full of them," Regis said.

"So what do you suppose he would make of this business Miss Spinelli told me about? Men getting a special kick out of doing it in the stunt shack?"

"Damn good question, Elvis," Regis said. "I imagine old Sigmund would have had a heyday with that one. It probably has to do with the danger factor—the risk of getting caught. Freud says that sex is both the strongest human drive and the biggest human taboo. You want to do it all the time, but you know you shouldn't. And somewhere along the way, the two get mixed up in your unconscious—the drive and the taboo—so that the bigger the taboo, the more exciting the sex. Kind of like the stunts themselves—the riskier they are, the more exciting they are to behold."

"Well, a scared dog'll get a hard-on—I *have* noticed that," Elvis said.

"Good point," Regis said. "Freud could have used that for a footnote. When it comes to sex, we all ain't nothin' but hound-dogs."

Elvis had to smile. He hadn't thought old Regis was the type to know his songs. "We men sure are a sorry lot, aren't we, Regis?" he said.

"Dr. Freud certainly thought so," Regis said, all seriousness again. "He says it all starts with our mothers. We love them so much that we want to marry them. But, of course, we can't and that's where all our problems begin. He says that's why we all end up with a Madonna-whore complex. We either treat women like our mothers—sainted ladies we wouldn't think of sleeping with. Or we treat them like whores. Nothing in between. That doesn't leave a whole lot of options for us, does it? Or for the women in our lives, for that matter."

"Baloney," Elvis said. "I think your Dr. Freud had sex on the brain."

Regis smiled. "He'd call that a defense. A defense for something that's troubling *you*."

"Well, maybe that's *his* defense for having sex on the brain," Elvis snapped.

Regis laughed. "Elvis, you would have made one hell of a lawyer!"

"Yup, that's my problem all right," Elvis said. "I missed my calling."

Both men laughed, and then fell quiet again.

"I'll tell you one thing, Elvis," Regis said after a few minutes. "Freud or no Freud, Holly McDougal was a victim long before she was murdered. Men forced her into whatever kind of life she led because men make the rules. Men run the show."

Elvis nodded. They had just passed the Lancaster town line and would be at the prison in less than ten minutes.

"How about you, Regis?" Elvis said, staring straight ahead. "You got woman problems?"

"I did," Regis said. "But I gave them up for Lent. Or maybe they gave up on me. Whichever, I've kept pretty much to myself for four or five years now."

"Don't you miss 'em?"

"Every minute of the day," Regis said.

They had to spend a good ten minutes with Warden Reardon before they got to see Squirm. Reardon wanted to talk about casting. Elvis, of course, would play Reardon himself. But how about Grace Kelly for his wife? A lot of people said Phoebe Reardon was the spitting image of Grace Kelly. But most important, he had this really crazy idea for Bobo Boyle, the goofy character doing time for passing bad checks. *Jerry Lewis!* Brilliant, wasn't it? Jerry Lewis as a con! Elvis agreed with everything.

When Squirm Littlejon saw Regis trail Elvis into the conference room, his face fell. He gave Elvis an enthusiastic hello, but only flicked an eye at Regis and then looked back to Elvis again. Elvis told Squirm that they had already made some progress in the case, but he didn't give any details. Then he said that they had to go over a part of Squirm's testimony at the trial that didn't jell with other evidence.

"You said those dress-up games with Miss Nancy never happened," Elvis said. "That she made the whole thing up."

Squirm did his shrinking thing again.

"Look me in the eye, Squirm," Elvis said. "You *did* play those games, didn't you?"

"I don't want to talk about it, Mr. Presley," Littlejon murmured.

Elvis smacked the metal table between them. "What the hell is wrong with you, boy? Would you rather spend your life in here than talk about—you know, talk about—"

"Sex," Regis chimed in.

"Right, sex," Elvis said quietly.

Squirm raised his manacled hands to his face, then leaned as far as he could across the table. "Can't talk with them around," he whispered, gesturing with his eyes toward the guards on either side of him.

Elvis looked at the guards, both of them burly men in short-sleeved shirts that revealed tattoos on their biceps—one celebrating the U.S. Marine Corps, the other celebrating someone named Lily.

"Gentleman, I'd be much obliged if I could have a couple of minutes of privacy with my client here," Elvis said.

"Can't do it, Elvis," the ex-marine said. "Regulations."

"Is it against regulations to accept my personal autograph?"

The guards conferred for a moment then headed for the door. "We'll be right outside," Lily's admirer said.

Littlejon squirmed around in his chair, his eyes cast down, and then began. "We'd been together about two years, living out at the beach house, and things started to cool down between us," he said quietly. "It's natural, I suppose. You still love each other, but the bed thing kind of loses its kick, if you know what I mean. So, after a while, you're doing it less and less. Kinda putting it off, like a chore. Well, that started to put Nanette in the dumps. She'd carry on about how I didn't find her attractive any more and I'd tell her I did, but, you know, actions speak louder than words."

Squirm stole a quick glance at Elvis then lowered his eyes again.

"Anyhow, she got ahold of this book called *Making Whoopie* by some sex doctor. And it was full of all kinds of tricks for what he called, 'rekindling the sexual fire.' Games and things. And one of them was this dress-up business—pretending you are somebody else to make it feel fresh."

"So that's when you suggested she dress up like Holly?" Elvis said.

"No," Squirm said. "I didn't even know who Holly was at that point. Never even seen her. But one day Nanette comes home with this schoolgirl get-up—little blouse and kilt and Mary Jane shoes. And to tell you the truth, it *did* turn me on. The sex doc was right, I guess."

It was the same kind of outfit that Nanette had seen Holly wear at the screen test—the screen test where Nanette was caught on film plainly seething with envy over the young girl's body.

"And who's idea was it to call her 'Holly' while you were—"

"Nanette's," Squirm said. "Like I said, I didn't even meet Holly until months after Nanette brought home that schoolgirl get-up."

"And when you *did* meet Holly . . . ?"

"She wasn't wearing anything like that when I met her, that's for sure," Squirm said. "First time she came out to the shack she was wearing some clingy thing that didn't leave a whole lot to the imagination. Tell you the truth, I never did think it was strange that her name was 'Holly,' like what Nanette wanted me to call her. It's a pretty common name. Just thought it was a coincidence."

"You're telling the truth now, Squirm," Elvis said softly.

"I swear," Littlejon said.

"And why didn't you tell the truth on the stand?"

Squirm shrugged. "It just didn't seem like, you know, the gentlemanly thing to do."

"Even after Nanette had told the whole court that the games were your idea?"

"That's right, Mr. Presley," Littlejon whispered.

"Well, you certainly are a gentleman, Squirm," Regis said. "One hell of a gentleman." These were the first words Regis had spoken since they entered the conference room, and there was not a trace of irony in his voice.

"One last thing," Elvis said. "Did you know that Holly McDougal was carrying on business in the stunt shack—call-girl business?"

Squirm raised his head, a tiny smirk playing on his lips. "You got to be kidding. That girl was giving it away."

"Only to special people," Regis said.

It was almost eleven o'clock before Elvis and Regis were back on the road again, heading for L.A. Elvis had signed his autograph for each of the guards—the ex-marine actually produced a little red autograph book—and then spent a few more minutes with Reardon discussing the possibility of casting Sidney Poitier as a death-row inmate. Elvis told him it was a fabulous idea, although this little charade was starting to make him feel kind of guilty.

Squirm's confession had given Elvis a strange feeling, part puzzlement, part disgust. God knows, there weren't any love songs out there about losing the desire to make love to the one you loved. No ballads about "rekindling the sexual fire," no "Dress-up Game Rock." Even if there were, he couldn't see himself singing them. Love was a pure and beautiful thing, not a psychological problem some sex doctor fixed up with a bag of tricks.

"So tell me, Regis, what was Nanette to Squirm—Madonna or whore?" Elvis kept his eyes on the road.

"Sounds like he tried to make her into both for a while there," Regis replied. "He wasn't turned on by this person he'd grown to love as a genuine woman, so she had to pretend to be somebody else for that part. At least until he found himself Holly to be his concubine."

Elvis shook his head. He wasn't buying it.

"In Europe, it's a way of life, at least for those who can afford it," Regis went on. "A Frenchman has his wife for raising his family and going to church with. And then he's got his mistress for the other. It's the accepted thing."

"Sounds like a lot of lying and cheating to me," Elvis said.

"I know what you mean," Regis said. "And that's why I dropped out of the whole game."

Elvis drove in silence for several minutes.

"How come you know so much about Dr. Freud?" Elvis said finally.

"At one point in my life I was trying to cure myself," Regis said.

"Of what?"

"Confusion," Regis replied.

15
AN ATTRACTION OF GENES

ELVIS slept for virtually the entire seven hours to Santa Teresa, only waking briefly to change from the commercial jet to a six-seater prop in Durango, then to a taxi and a bus in Tuxpap. Even though his ankle was no longer throbbing, he had taken an entire tablet of painkiller in Los Angeles Airport just in case it flared up again. In any event, the pill made the time pass pleasantly enough. It carried him off to a country of the mind where the landscape was unobstructed and there were no choices to be made.

Dr. Hector Garcia was waiting for them at the Santa Teresa bus stop with a cup of piping hot *café con leche* in each hand, an amazing feat considering that the bus had arrived over an hour late. Garcia was a slight man with a graying goatee and glittering black eyes. His English was heavily accented, but perfectly understandable, Judge Lowenstein's ruling to the contrary. Elvis liked Garcia immediately.

The instituto was only a short walk away. You could see it from the bus stop, a complex of pink missionary-style buildings in the midst of tin shacks, all surrounded by towering tropical mountains. Regis and Garcia walked ahead, talking animatedly in Spanish, while Elvis lingered behind, sipping his coffee and breathing in the fragrant jungle air. He felt like he had awakened from one dream into another. It was a bit like Hawaii here, but a whole lot wilder. He had never seen such starkly vibrant colors as in these tropical flowers and trees, never moved through air so light and invisible, or experienced such profound silence. The faint sputter of the bus, now a good mile away, sounded grotesquely artificial, an affront to nature. For one delirious moment, Elvis could not remember exactly what had brought him here, but it did not matter in the least. He felt free and at peace. Why would a man want anything more than that?

He followed Garcia and Regis into a building where the temperature immediately dropped and the noise level rose. Intense-looking young men and women in laboratory coats were scurrying through the corridors, clipboards and notebooks in hand. Some looked up and smiled, but most remained hunched over, jabbering to one another in Spanish at warp speed. Near the end of the corridor, Garcia stopped and pushed open a door, holding it for his guests.

If Santa Teresa was an explosion of nature in the raw, Dr. Hector Garcia's laboratory was a monument to the clean lines and sterile spaces wrought by the hand of man. *Another world within a world*, Elvis thought. Which one is real? Selma had once read him a Japanese fable about a man who dreams that he is a butterfly; when he awakes, he wonders if he is a butterfly dreaming that he is a man.

"Mr. Clifford, I wish you to meet my colleague, Dr. Suarez," Garcia was saying.

A dark-haired woman in a lab coat offered her hand to Regis. Dr. Suarez was in her late thirties, olive-skinned, with an oval face and pronounced cheekbones. Elvis looked at Regis. The man looked positively stunned, as if he had just been stung by some narcotic jungle flower. The expression on the woman's face immediately changed too, softening and brightening at the same time. They took one another's hands and for one suspended moment, just stood there, looking at one another in nothing short of wonderment.

There was not a doubt in Elvis's mind about what was happening right in front of his eyes. By God, he was witnessing a man and a woman falling in love on the spot. It was a phenomenon that was exalted in hundreds of songs—he'd sung a fair share of them himself—but he had never actually seen it happen before. The truth was, he had always thought it was just another songwriter's fantasy, a dream to give the listeners hope, although Elvis believed that it actually made most listeners feel cheated by life. *I never fell in love like that*, they thought. *And I never will.*

But just a minute here—*Regis?* The man who had sworn off women? The man who seemed to hope for nothing more than a few hundred dollars and a bottle of Scotch? What the devil was going on here? Was it something in the tropical air? Had Dr. Garcia slipped Regis some potion he had concocted in his jungle laboratory? Elvis looked over at Garcia—he looked just as startled and enchanted as Elvis was. Elvis felt his heart swell. Life seemed full of possibilities.

"I am all set up for you, Mr. Presley," Garcia said, gesturing toward a large stainless-steel apparatus at the far end of the laboratory.

Leaving Regis and Dr. Suarez talking softly to one another, Elvis followed Garcia to what turned out to be a high-intensity microscope. Garcia presented Elvis with a diagram that laid out his findings: not only had he separated the two emission samples from the victim's swab, but later—*after* the trial—he had taken a third sample directly from Frederick Littlejon in prison.

Garcia had done this on his own, not even telling Clifford about it. Dyed and magnified, Littlejon's sample matched one of those from the swab—the more degraded emission; in other words, the *earlier* one. Garcia's conclusion was clear: Holly McDougal definitely had had sexual intercourse with the second man four to six hours *after* she had been with Littlejon.

"Please. I wish you to see with your own eyes," Garcia said as he placed two glass slides onto the microscope stage. He guided Elvis to the binocular eyepieces. "On the left is Mr. Littlejon, on the right, the other man. The mystery man. Without doubt, the murderer."

As Elvis gazed at the two circles filled with worm-like squiggles, he felt pleasantly dizzy. Here was yet another world within a world. If Man had been born with lenses like these for his eyes, *this* would be his real world and the other—faces and mountains and trees—would be the invisible world that only the scientists could see with their powerful tools.

"Notice the length of the tails," Garcia was saying. "Shorter, stubbier on the left. That is from age. These cells age by minutes and hours, not by years."

One slide slipped away and another slid into view.

"DNA," Garcia said. "The blueprint of all the cells in a body. These are Mr. Littlejon's. There is not another in the entire world of three billion people that is exactly like his."

Elvis pulled back from the eyepieces and looked at Garcia. "Are you sure about all this, Doctor?"

"Very," Garcia replied. "What you are looking at is infinitely more exact than a fingerprint. A strand of hair, a speck of tissue, a teardrop—any one of these is enough to match with one human being and one only."

Elvis felt his heart accelerate.

"So it's a done deal, Doc!" he blurted. "We got it all right here—proof positive that Littlejon is innocent. Let's just pack it up and take it to a judge!"

Garcia responded with a rueful smile. "It is proof to us, but it is nothing in a court of law," he said. "Not in any country. It seems my little laboratory in the middle of the jungle is, how you say, ahead of its time. But in our work, we learn patience. Perhaps in forty years, our findings will be acceptable as evidence."

"In forty years Squirm will be an old man, Doctor."

"That is true, Mr. Presley," Garcia said. "It is also true that there are thousands of other people in prison for crimes they did not commit. And I could prove it so right now, but no one would believe me."

"Guess we'll just have to set up our own little country then." It was Regis speaking. He and Dr. Suarez had quietly stepped behind Elvis, and now Dr. Suarez was laughing softly at Regis's little witticism, the generous laugh of the devoted.

"Hold on," Elvis said. "Does all this mean that you could match the second emission with just one person, Doctor? With the murderer?"

"Yes, I could do that right now if I had a cell of the murderer. But I do not, of course. And, anyway, as I say, that would not mean anything in a court of law."

"But suppose we did get cells from other folks," Elvis said. "You know, people we suspected. If you could make a match with the last person Miss McDougal was with, we'd know we had our man. Wouldn't stand up in court, but at least we'd know exactly where to look real careful for something that did."

"That is an excellent thought, Mr. Presley," Garcia said.

"But how, pray tell, do you go about getting people's cells?" Regis said. "Follow them around with a scalpel and nick off a little chunk of their earlobes when they aren't looking?"

"Well, you could make them cry and catch their teardrops," Elvis said.

Dr. Garcia beamed at Elvis. "Mr. Presley, have you ever considered going into forensic medicine? You have a natural talent for it."

"I'll keep it in mind," Elvis said.

Garcia led Elvis to a laboratory bench where he showed him how to take and preserve cell samples without corrupting them. He put together a little kit for him of eyedroppers, tweezers, blotting paper, vials, and suspensory fluid. Regis watched for most of the demonstration then wandered off with Dr. Suarez to the other side of the laboratory. Elvis looked after them. He winked at Garcia.

"Does Dr. Suarez have this effect on a lot of men?" he asked quietly.

"I have known Dolores—Dr. Suarez—for fifteen years and I have never seen anything like this. She is all work and no play, which is good for the laboratory, of course," Garcia said, smiling.

"And Mr. Clifford? Is he a—"

"The man just told me yesterday that he swore off women five years ago."

"This is a beautiful thing to behold, is it not?" Garcia said, looking at the couple.

"Does make a man wonder," Elvis said, grinning.

"Perhaps it is encoded in their DNA," Garcia said. "An attraction of genes."

"They could've gone their whole lives never meeting each other."

"Or perhaps it had to happen," Garcia said. "Perhaps the attraction in their genes is so strong that it drew them together across thousands of miles."

The four of them made arrangements to meet for dinner at Santa Teresa's one and only restaurant at eight that evening. In the meantime, Dr. Suarez said she would show Regis around the campus, and Dr. Garcia apologized for having to return to an experiment in progress. He gave Elvis directions to the institute's botanical gardens, the best in all of Central America, he said.

The gardens were a marvel, all right, an entire walled-in acre of tropical vegetation so lush and vibrant that it gave Elvis a raw feeling, like his skin was too pale and thin to abide with it. He limped over to a white iron bench and let himself down gently. His ankle had started up again; it seemed to get worse when he was alone. He broke off half a painkiller and chewed it down. In front of him, a brilliant red blossom the size of a man's head wagged back and forth in a nonexistent breeze. Elvis had the distinct feeling that it was trying to tell him something. . . .

It was ten minutes to eight when Elvis awoke. As he opened his eyes, the red flower head was still swaying in front of him, but something about it had changed. Its outer petals had begun to curl inward toward the center, giving it a contented, sleepy-eyed look. Little wonder—it had been chatting to Elvis nonstop while he slept.

Regis and Delores Suarez were waltzing cheek to cheek to the strains of a marimba band on the jukebox as Elvis limped into the Cafe con Pep Moso. Dr. Garcia waved to him from a table by the wall. It was already covered with little serving plates of food—guacamole, refried beans, yellow rice with bits of red pepper and pork in it, bright green peas, barbecued ribs, slices of mango—along with a pitcher of sangria. By the time Elvis had made his way to the table, Garcia had ladled small portions of each food in a colorful circle on Elvis's plate like a painter's palette.

"Did you enjoy the gardens?" Garcia asked as Elvis sat down.

"I surely did," Elvis said. "One of them flowers talked my ear off."

Garcia smiled. "They get lonely for human company," he said.

Elvis absently dipped a slice of mango into the guacamole and stuck it in his mouth. The meat of the fruit had a soft, silky texture that slipped languidly on his tongue, coasting on the slick of the avocado dip. Now there was something he'd never thought about before: how food *feels* in his mouth. It was a whole other thing, separate from taste or hunger. And it was a glorious thing for sure. You just had to pay attention to it. How many other things in life had he missed just for lack of paying attention?

One juke box song ended, another began, and Regis and Delores were still dancing. They were in love all right; you didn't have to pay too much attention to see that. There was nothing elegant about the way they moved, nothing that dazzled the eye, but they danced totally *together*—two people, one motion. Just the opposite of the way most people danced these days, which was two people, two totally different performances. That's just what it was now, wasn't it? *Performances.* Two people strutting their stuff for each other like dancing was an advertisement for themselves. That's what Holly McDougal's dance on the screen test had been all about. *Look at me! Desire me! Yearn for me!* Heck, wasn't that what Elvis's own gyrating performances were really all about too?

But, at this moment, sitting in the Cafe con Pep Moso in the middle of the Mexican tropics, the last thing in the world that Elvis wanted to do was perform. No, right now, listening to the Spanish music, breathing in the flower- and food-scented air, watching the two lovers meld into one another's arms, Elvis was simply a Watcher and a Listener. Not putting anything *out*, just taking everything *in*. And, O Lord, what a pleasure that was.

"Mr. Clifford tells me that you are a twin also," Garcia was saying.

"That's right," Elvis replied, turning to his table mate. "But my twin, Jesse Garon, he died when we were born."

"Yes, I understand," Garcia said. "You are the exceptions, you know. Identical twins have exactly the same DNA. The same genetic blueprint, the same genetic fingerprint."

Elvis nodded and looked back at the dancers, but something was tugging at his mind, that half-formed embryo of a question that had skittered across his consciousness just before he fell asleep the other night.

"Dr. Garcia, how much do twins have to do with each other when—you know—when they are still inside their mom?"

"A great deal, in my opinion," Garcia said seriously. "Especially in the third trimester when they are very close to being fully-formed human beings. They are locked together in the same little space for every second of every day. Always touching. When one moves, the other must move also. It would be impossible for them not to be aware of each other. In fact, I would say that there is nothing else that they *are* aware of."

"So I knew Jesse," Elvis said, looking deeply into Garcia's eyes. "I knew he was there."

"In some way, yes," Garcia said. "But we cannot begin to understand what that way could be. What an unborn child's consciousness is like. I imagine it is a murky thing, that he does not really know where his body ends and the other body begins. Perhaps the unborn child has that consciousness that holy men seek—where all things are one thing."

"But I knew he was there," Elvis repeated anxiously. "I probably even had feelings about him."

"Perhaps," Garcia said.

"Unconscious feelings?" Elvis asked softly, his heart beating rapidly.

Hector Garcia studied Elvis with his shinning black eyes for several moments before he responded.

"You had absolutely nothing to do with your twin's premature death, Mr. Presley," he said quietly. "I can assure you of that."

"But there are no accidents, are there?" Elvis said.

"I am a scientist," Garcia said. "And in my opinion, there is nothing in the universe *but* accidents."

16
PEACE IN THE VALLEY

THEY were in the air, jetting out of Durango the next morning, before Elvis brought up the subject of Dr. Dolores Suarez.

"You serious about this woman, Regis?"

Regis gazed out at the clouds for a moment.

"Or it's just a dream," he said.

"Well, I was there and it didn't look like a dream to me," Elvis said, grinning. "I never seen anything quite like it. You were dancing to the same music the minute you laid eyes on each other."

"That's the truth," Regis said. "It doesn't make any sense, but it's the truth."

"I'm real happy for you, Regis," Elvis said.

"Thank you, Elvis," Regis said. He again looked out the airplane window for a moment, then, "I owe it all to you, you know. My whole life seems to have spun around a hundred and eighty degrees since you walked into my office."

Just another accident, Elvis thought, but he didn't say anything. A stewardess leaned over their seats. "May I get you something to drink, senors?" she asked.

"No, thank you, ma'am," Elvis said.

Regis hesitated, biting down on his lip. "Okay," he said finally. "A tequila sunrise, if you don't mind." But as the stewardess walked on, he looked earnestly into Elvis's face and said, "It's my last drink, you know. That part of my life is over too."

"Glad to hear that, Regis."

Elvis didn't stay awake long enough to see if Regis actually did limit himself to a single tequila sunrise; he slipped the other half of the painkiller into his mouth and slept all the way to L.A. At the airport, Elvis stuffed another three-day advance into Regis's pocket and gave him Dr. Garcia's cell-gathering kit for safekeeping. Regis said he would get to work on the Holly McDougal safety deposit box problem immediately, then jumped into a cab. Elvis got behind the wheel of his Eldorado and headed west for Nevada.

The Sparks Harvest Festival and Rodeo was winding down its last day by the time Elvis arrived that evening. In the parking area, trailers were loading up with horses and cattle, and men and women in coveralls were wrestling game stalls and dismantled fair rides onto flatbeds. All the carnival gizmos and rodeo paraphernalia and wiry bodies reminded Elvis of the stunt shack on the MGM lot; it sure seemed a natural thing to pop back and forth between those two worlds.

But busy as everybody at the Sparks Rodeo was, they all stopped and stared the moment Elvis got out of his car and braced his crutches under his shoulders. For a long moment, the parking lot went hushed as a prairie, and then one of the young men in overalls yodeled out, "Whoopee! It's Elvis!" and soon they were all cheering and yelling and surging toward him with big happy grins on their faces. Elvis smiled back at them, feeling gratified and more than a little wistful. Man, he hadn't been at a rodeo or county fair since the old days when he did fairground shows with Jimmie Rogers Snow in Lubbock and Rosewell and Bastrop. This here was a long way from Hollywood—or Vegas, for that matter. Elvis felt a real and instant connection with these folks.

"What brings you to Sparks, Elvis?" the yodeler asked, slapping Elvis on the shoulder.

"I come to pay my respects to Will Cathcart," Elvis replied. His response filtered back through the crowd in a rolling murmur.

"Awful thing," one of the coveralled young women said. "'Specially for his widow and young 'uns."

"That it is," Elvis said. "She here?"

"Yup, that's her over by the bandstand," the young woman said, pointing. "They're puttin' together a benefit, you know. A little butter and egg money to get 'em started on their own."

Squinting, Elvis saw a sandy-haired girl in a white cotton dress that bulged out at the belly. She didn't look more than seventeen or eighteen. On either side of her, grasping at her skirts, were towheaded toddlers.

"That why you're here, Elvis?" someone asked. "For the benefit?" Elvis looked out at the crowd that now completely encircled him, and they looked back at him with one bright and honest expectant face. It was only an accident that he was here at this exact moment, but maybe that was the deal with accidents: you had to know what to do with them.

"Yes," Elvis said. "That's why I'm here."

The entire group streamed toward the bandstand with Elvis limping at its center. Along the way, others attached themselves in twos and threes, and by the time they reached Will's widow, Jilly-Jo Cathcart, their number had doubled. The swarm parted to let Jilly-Jo and her two children in. All three of them looked as if they had been doing more crying than breathing in the last couple of days.

"I'm very sorry for you, ma'am," Elvis said, offering Jilly-Jo his hand.

"Kind of you," the young woman answered in a whisper, her eyes cast down. She only touched Elvis's hand for a second, then pulled it away and set it back on the shoulder of her youngest.

"I just made Will's acquaintance a few days back," Elvis went on. "But he struck me as a fine young man."

"Will told me 'bout that," Jilly-Jo said. "He was sorry, you know—" She gestured with her head at Elvis's ankle.

"No matter at all," Elvis said. "He was not to blame."

"'Course not," she said. "It was Mickey. He runs the show."

"Mickey Grieves?"

Jilly-Jo leaned her head close to Elvis's ear. "He's a bad man, Mr. Presley, and I done told him so to his face. Day before yesterday."

"He was here, at Sparks?"

The young woman nodded.

"Ma'am, was he here *before* Will's accident?" Elvis asked urgently.

"Yes," she whispered, looking as if she was about to cry again.

Above them, on the bandstand, two young men were tuning up their electric guitars. Between them, an older guy with a bandana wrapped around his head was adjusting his electric fiddle and behind him was a rail-thin girl in a denim shirt and overalls bracing a standing bass against her shoulder. At the edge of the crowd, a cheer went up. Cars and pickups and even one big old school bus were suddenly streaming in from every which direction, kicking up clouds of dust, their windows open and people shouting out through them. "Elvis!" echoed from the vehicles to the bandstand crowd and back again. The word was out in Sparks, Nevada.

Elvis asked Jilly-Jo if they could talk again later, then limped his way to the bandstand steps. Two young roustabouts appeared on either side of Elvis; someone took his crutches and then the two young men made a four-handed seat, carried him to center stage, and set him down on a high-standing stool behind a microphone. The roar that greeted him was about as thunderous and joyful as any he'd heard. Elvis bowed his head and held it down for several minutes.

When the din finally quieted, Elvis raised his head, looked out and smiled. The entire fairgrounds was packed, virtually all the people standing, their faces turned up to him. Behind him, the fiddle player murmured, "More folks than we've had here three days runnin'." Elvis motioned to him, whispered something in his ear, then turned back to the audience.

"This here is for Will and Jilly-Jo," he said into the microphone.

The fiddler sawed off a plaintive introduction and then Elvis stood up straight and began to sing "Love Me Tender." Behind him, the bass joined in on the beat after "Never let me go," followed by the two guitars at the end of the first verse.

It had been awhile since Elvis had sung the song, but it came out of him with more genuine feeling than he could remember ever giving it. Something was stirring inside of him—an awful ache for this dear young widow child and the awkward young man who was lost to her forever—and it found its way into the heart of his voice. By the time he reached, "I'll be yours through all the years, till the end of time," there were tears rolling down Elvis's cheeks. The fiddler closed with a minor-key reprise of his intro and then, for several seconds, the only sound that could be heard at the Sparks Harvest Festival and Rodeo were the sniffles and swallows of the assembled guests. Someone finally broke the silence with a soft hand clap, another joined in, then another, and finally the whole field from the bandstand to the stables to the empty, revolving Ferris wheel was clapping loud and long and steady. Not a voice was raised; this was the applause of deep and humble respect.

"There are going to be hats passing among you," Elvis finally said into the microphone. "You know what to do, folks."

Immediately, upturned Stetson hats began radiating from the front row out into the crowd. Elvis conferred with the fiddler again, then asked one of the guitarists if he could borrow his Fender for the next number.

"Thank you, thank you very much," Elvis said. "This next one I want to dedicate to my friend Regis Clifford and his woman, Delores Suarez. She's a doctor, folks. My friend Regis has landed himself a doctor."

A ripple of giggles went through the crowd and then they went quiet as Elvis launched into "Young Dreams." Again, the song came out of him pure as honey, as he thought about Regis and Delores pushing into their forties but with a sudden love as young as any twenty-year-old's. God, it was a pleasure to sing from the heart again.

The crowd roared, the Stetsons came back front chock full of paper money, somebody emptied the hats into a barrel, and out they went again as Elvis came to the microphone for the next song, "Teddy Bear."

"I dedicate this one to my best buddy, Billy Jackson. Looks like a nice woman has taken a fancy to him. Love is alive and well, folks, thank the Lord!"

As Elvis came to, "I don't wanna be a tiger/'Cause tigers play too rough," he pantomimed a tiger clawing at the air, his hips doing a slithery jungle thing. The crowd laughed and started clapping rhythmically right through, "I don't wanna be a lion/'Cause lions ain't the kind you love enough." The fact that Elvis was bouncing around on his sprained ankle did not even occur to him. He was having too much fun.

When he dedicated the next song, "Jailhouse Rock," to Squirm Littlejon, "an innocent man who's doing time for being at the wrong place at the wrong time," many people in the audience kind of gasped, while others let out a cheer of "Squirm!" Rodeo folks, at least, hadn't forgotten about the case of Squirm Littlejon.

By the end of this number, the barrel was pretty much full and somebody rolled out another one as the hats went out again. Elvis conferred with the fiddler and came back to the microphone.

"This here is my last one, friends," he said. "And I'm sending it out to every man and woman who ever lost a loved one. It's the heartbreak that never heals, folks. *Never.* So this one is to the memory of Will Cathcart . . . and—" Elvis stopped and swallowed hard. "And it's to the memory of Miss Selma DuPres."

The fiddler jumped right in with the intro to "There Will Be Peace in the Valley for Me" and once again Elvis found himself singing the truth in the song, the heart at its center.

> *Oh well, I'm tired and so weary*
> *But I must go alone*
> *Till the Lord comes and calls, calls me away, oh yes*
> *Well the morning's so bright*
> *And the lamp is alight*
> *And the night, night is as black as the sea, oh yes*

As he sang on, Elvis's mind jumped from an image of that moment when he witnessed Regis and Delores falling in love to the sound of Connie Spinelli's voice when she asked if Billy was married, and from there to the sadness in Jilly-Jo Cathcart's eyes and then to Selma's warm smile as she led him into her bedroom in Alamo, Tennessee. God, yes, love was alive and well, and even if his heart was breaking, it was full—yes, full of love. But as he came to the reprise, he realized that not once had an image of Priscilla come to him. Or of Ann-Margret. In fact, he had not thought about either of them in days.

> *There will be peace in the valley for me, some day*
> *There will be peace in the valley for me, oh Lord I pray*
> *There'll be no sadness, no sorrow*
> *No trouble, trouble I see*
> *There will be peace in the valley for me, for me*

In front of the bandstand, folks were now moving on in an orderly file from left to right, digging deep into their pockets and handbags and tossing even more money into the barrels, then looking up at Elvis and smiling and saluting before continuing out to the parking lot. For a long, soulful moment, Elvis was back at Ray Kaserne in Friedberg, Germany, singing "Silent Night" to the enlisted men setting off on Christmas leave, and the love he felt in his heart surged out to every man, woman, and child passing in front of him. Yes, for one long wonder-filled moment, Elvis once again remembered exactly why it was that he had always wanted to be a singer.

The total in the barrels came to $1,273 and Elvis added a check for $3,727, "just to make it come out even," as he said to Jilly-Jo Cathcart after the concert was over. They talked a bit longer, but she had nothing more to add about Mickey Grieves, and she told Elvis that Will had never mentioned anything to her about a Holly McDougal or Squirm Littlejon. She had no idea what it was that Will had intended to tell Elvis once he got back from the rodeo. Finally, Jilly-Jo said that Will's funeral was out in Maywood tomorrow at eleven and Elvis was welcome to come.

The crowd around Elvis had thinned down to just a couple dozen, including the two roustabouts who had carried him up to the bandstand. He asked one of them if they could show him exactly where the bull had gored Will Cathcart to death and again the crowd moved with them, like bees around a Queen Bee, to the main-event corral. There was nothing much to see there—no blood, no scraps of clothing. Less than an hour after Will's body had been carted off, the bull-wrassling competition had continued on the same spot. All in a day's work. Now one of the roustabouts leaned in to Elvis's ear.

"Want to see the bull?" he asked.

"Yup."

The young man led Elvis to a stable just outside the corral's far end. At its entrance, he told Elvis that it would be better if they went in alone; Elvis asked the crowd to excuse him for a bit and they stayed behind respectfully. Then he swung on his crutches over the hay-strewn floor to a stall by the wall. The roustabout swung open the stall door. There lay a Celtic shorthorn of easily nine hundred pounds. It was dead.

"They kill him right after?" Elvis asked.

"Would have," the young man said. "You always kill the bull who kills a man. But didn't have to this time."

"How's that?"

"Bull died on his own just a few minutes after."

"What from?"

"Don't know. Just keeled over dead right next to young Will."

"That ever happen before?"

"Only once. Turned out the bull had a bad case of high blood pressure—made him go crazy and then have a heart attack."

Elvis set a foot on the bull's rear shank.

"Would you do me a favor?" he said. "Get a vet over here and find out what killed him. I'll foot the bill."

Elvis pulled a roll of bills out of his pocket and started to peel off fifty-dollars worth, but the young man held up both palms in a gesture of refusal.

"This one's on me, Elvis," the young man said. "We never can repay you for what you done today."

Elvis gave the roustabout Regis's phone number and told him to call after the vet did his autopsy.

By the time Elvis pulled in to the Stardust Cabins near Yosemite, he could barely keep his eyes open. It was just a little past midnight and he'd intended to drive all the way back to L.A., but the minute he got behind the wheel, his ankle had started to throb worse than ever—that prancing around on the bandstand hadn't done it any good—so he'd chewed down a painkiller and, soon enough, he'd been doing the vehicular equivalent of sleepwalking.

The check-in clerk was an old guy in an Indian-rug bathrobe who looked like he'd just woken up and wasn't too happy about it. He didn't appear to recognize Elvis, but after they'd done the paperwork he said, simply, "You done good in Sparks, Elvis," and then rambled back to his La-Z-Boy recliner.

As soon as he entered his cabin, Elvis switched on the TV for company, then flopped down on the bed with his boots on. He was out in a minute.

Elvis's dream came in fits and scraps. One minute he's singing "Love Me Tender" to a herd of bulls, the next he's doing the wash with his mother at the Laundromat in Tupelo. Doing it with Rinso and singing the Rinso White ditty with the box in his hand. It was one of those dreams where he knew he was dreaming and the thought popped into his head that this Rinso business was product placement—*product placement in his own dream!* Now who in heck had arranged that—the Colonel? The dream bounced on: Regis dancing the tango with Delores in the Santa Teresa Botanical Garden, but when Regis swung around you could see that half his cheek was gone, and his right eye was hanging out by a thread. Except that it wasn't his eye, it was Elvis himself, dangling from the ceiling by the Stuntman's Mistress. "Mr. Presley was allegedly spotted singing at a rodeo today in Sparks, Nevada, adding one more twist to the mystery of his disappearance."

Elvis's eyes fluttered open.

"For more on this breaking story, we go to Rich Fitzpatrick in Hollywood."

"Bill, I'm standing here with Patrolman Tom Schultz of the LAPD. Officer Schultz is the last person to have seen Elvis since he slipped away from the MGM studios Tuesday afternoon."

Elvis pulled himself up against the headboard and squinted at the TV.

"I'll tell you, Rich," Schultz was saying. "Elvis looked strange, real strange. Eyes all bleary, like he'd been crying. Face red. And he was real agitated. Like I said, he was doing ninety miles an hour when I pulled him over, and first thing he does is start talking about recording this duet with Hank Snow, right there in his car."

"Incredible," the reporter said. "Tell me, Officer Schultz, in your opinion had Mr. Presley been drinking?"

Schultz bit down on his lip. "No, not *drinking*," he murmured tentatively.

"Are you suggesting that he'd been taking drugs, Officer?"

"That's not for me to say, is it?" Schultz said.

"Back to you, Bill."

Elvis rubbed his eyes. No, he was awake all right. So what the devil was going on here? Exactly how long *had* he been away from his house on Perugia Way? Tonight, here, last night in Santa Teresa, and the night before with Regis. Three nights and he's a missing person?

"One unconfirmed report has even placed Elvis in London, holed up in the Cummington Arms Hotel with his latest Hollywood conquest, Ann-Margret," reporter Bill was saying.

Elvis rolled out of bed, hopped over to the TV and snapped it off.

Damn every last one of them! He limped back to the bed and picked up the telephone receiver from the bed table, but immediately dropped it back onto its cradle. Who the heck was he going to call anyway? The Colonel, so he could take some abuse for not reporting his whereabouts every minute of the day? Priscilla, so he could listen to her weep while he assured her that he was not holed up in London with Ann-Margret?

He pulled off his boots and lay back in the bed. He felt a smile creep up on his lips before he realized what put it there. Man, it felt good to be a missing person. It was probably the closest thing to freedom he could hope for anymore. Selma had once told him about a famous writer who faked his death and changed his name just so he could get his own life back.

This time when Elvis closed his eyes, he was blessed with a dreamless sleep that was all music.

17

SUFFOCATING DEMON

"IT'S ALL over, Elvis! *Done! The end!*"

Regis was standing unsteadily in the doorway to his office with a glass of Scotch in his hand when Elvis came hobbling up the stairs the next morning. Regis looked like he had been drinking since daybreak; so much for the resolutions of new-found love.

"What the devil is wrong with you, man?" Elvis limped up to Regis and made a grab for his glass of booze, but Regis swung it away, spilling half its contents in the process.

"I tell you, it's over!" Regis yanked a folded *Los Angeles Times* out of his jacket pocket and thrust it in front of Elvis's face. "Read all about it! You *both* made the front page, big guy!"

Elvis grabbed the paper and limped over to the window. The lead story was about the FBI's preliminary report on the Birmingham church bombing and the second lead was about President Kennedy's upcoming visit to Dallas; sandwiched in between were two short news columns. The one on the left was headlined "The King Surfaces: Elvis at Sparks Rodeo Benefit." And the headline right next to it was "Killer Escapes CCI: Littlejon Squirms Loose."

"God Almighty!" Elvis cried. "When did this happen?"

"Middle of the night," Regis said.

"How'd Squirm do it?"

"How do you think, movie star? It was a set-up. Somebody on the inside showed him right to the door. They *wanted* him to escape!"

"It says that here?" Elvis scanned down the article.

"Of course not!" Regis blasted. "Your pal Reardon says they took Squirm to the prison infirmary in the middle of the night because he was complaining of chest pains. They turned their backs and, *abracadabra*, he's gone. And if you believe that, pal, I've got a nice deal for you on the Golden Gate Bridge."

"It could've happened that way," Elvis said. "Squirm's a slippery guy. That's how he got his name."

"He's slippery, but he's no magician," Regis said. "One thing Reardon fails to mention is that there hasn't been an escape from CCI in thirty-two years. Tight as a drum. Why now? Why Squirm and nobody else? I'm telling you, it was a set-up."

"But why in heck would they *want* him to escape?"

"So they can track him down and shoot him, no questions asked," Regis said. "The giveaway is that Reardon insists that Squirm is armed and dangerous. The Singing Warden doesn't have a clue how Squirm escaped, but he's dead sure he's got a gun. And that, my friend, is license to kill him on the spot."

"Why the heck do they want to kill him? They had him locked up for life."

"Because that'll put an end to any questions the public has," Regis said. "Nobody ever believes an escaped con is innocent. *Never.* They figure he wouldn't run if he was innocent. This way, the case gets put to rest for good. Escaped killer shot, end of story. Squirm was an idiot for going along with it, for thinking they were really just letting him get away scot-free. Now he'll be a dead idiot."

"But he's a convicted man, Regis!" Elvis bellowed. "Nobody gives a hoot what the public thinks about him."

"Not before they didn't. But they do now. Ever since last night when the King of Rock 'n' Roll decided to become a social protester. *Mister* Joan Baez. Suddenly, the whole world is talking about Squirm Littlejon." Regis pointed a shaky finger at the article that Mike Murphy had written in the *Times* about Elvis.

Elvis skimmed down the story:

> . . . Elvis dedicated his next song, "Jailhouse Rock," to Squirm Littlejon *(see adjoining story)*, declaring that the convicted murderer of actress Holly McDougal was innocent, "a man who was simply at the wrong place at the wrong time."

Anonymous sources have informed the *Times* that Mr. Presley is currently sponsoring a private investigation of the Littlejon case with the intention of reopening it. Apparently, Presley believes that Mr. Littlejon was framed for the crime and that the guilty party is still at large. Presley's investigation may, in fact, account for his mysterious absence during the past three days.

"That was a dumb mistake, I guess," Elvis said quietly.

"You bet it was, movie star!" Regis retorted mercilessly. "As soon as Littlejon became a *cause celebre*, somebody decided to act fast. And, God damnit, they did! They set him up like turkey in a barrel."

Elvis hobbled over to the chair across from Regis's desk and sat down heavily.

"I'm sorry, Regis," he said. "I got carried away by all that feeling over there in Sparks. I dedicated a love song to you and Delores too."

"How touching," Regis intoned sarcastically as he filled his glass again. "That's over too, you know. Who the hell did I think I was kidding? A second chance for Regis Clifford? The drunk falls in love and turns over a new leaf? Sounds like some cornball country ditty. Give it to your songwriters, pal. You can make another million."

Elvis felt himself flinch inside. What in the name of God was he doing taking this abuse from a bitter, drunken bum he'd only met a few days ago? He'd gone out of his way to help the poor guy, for godssake—way out of his way. Given him money, given him hope. And this was the pay-off? It was bad enough that Regis had forgotten who he was talking to, but had Elvis forgotten himself? He was *Elvis Presley*, for godssake! Regis Clifford was lucky he even gave him the time of day.

Elvis felt a sickness in his gut. He reached for his crutches. Regis was right about one thing: it was over, all right. All over. Once they tracked down Squirm—once they *shot* him—no one would have the stomach to reopen his case. Not a single judge in the entire state of California would risk disclosing that not only had they jailed the wrong man, but they had killed him too. That is exactly the kind of public disaster that the people in charge will do absolutely anything to avoid—including burying the truth along with Squirm Littlejon.

"Here's your money back, movie star. Nobody can say Regis Clifford ever kept a nickel he didn't earn."

Regis flung some crumpled bills onto his desk. Elvis gathered them up and stuck them in his pocket without looking at Regis. Then he braced himself onto his crutches and started for the door. That awful feeling in his gut was getting worse, reaching up to his chest and making it hard for him to breathe. He was in the corridor now. He glanced up and there he was again in Doc Goldstein's mirror: Elvis Presley, the King of Rock'n'Roll, limping along a dingy hallway in West Hollywood with two days' growth on his face. The misbegotten twin. The *loser* twin. Well, damn it, Regis could have that role all to himself. Elvis had better things to do with his life.

Elvis looped his right arm through both crutches, then braced his hands on the handrail and started hopping down the stairs, the tips of his crutches bouncing on the steps behind him. Okay, so Colonel was right—he wasn't cut out for this line of work. He'd been greedy to think he was. The good Lord had made him a superstar, wasn't that enough? All this snoop business gave you was a lame foot and an abusive partner. And let's face it, Elvis had done more harm than good these past few days. Some *real* harm too. Like if Will Cathcart really was murdered, that was on Elvis's head. That surely wouldn't have happened if he hadn't stuck his nose in.

Elvis halted on the stairs, gasping for breath. *God forgive me!* He hadn't actually thought about it that way before: *Jilly-Jo Cathcart was a widow because of him!* Her husband had been about to give him incriminating evidence, so they shut him up for good. And now Squirm too—he'd be sitting in prison, but at least he'd still be alive if Elvis hadn't butted in. *God help me, I've done terrible harm!*

Elvis limped slowly down the rest of the stairs, pushed open the door to the street, and drew in a lung full of fresh air. A Latin beat pulsed out of the open door of the record shop. Elvis leaned on his crutches, listening. It was one of those heroic-sounding Spanish numbers with a wailing solo trumpet. The horn sounded sorrowful and brave at the same time, like a bull fighter who's down and bleeding bad, but won't give up—not yet. Not *ever*.

If Elvis just walked away from this whole rotten business, Holly McDougal's murderer could rest easy for the rest of his life. Same for whoever turned Jilly-Jo Cathcart into a teenage widow. *Now what kind of man turned his back on that?*

Elvis spun around. He left his crutches leaning against the outside wall, hobbled back up the stairs, and stumbled into Regis's office.

"It ain't over, Regis!" he bellowed. "None of it!"

Regis looked up at him from his desk, a sneer plastered on his plastered face. He was drinking straight from the bottle now. Elvis lunged across the desk and smacked the bottle out of his hand. It bounced off the wall and shattered on the floor. Regis cringed, his hands flying up in front of his face like a terrified child.

"You're a quitter, man!" Elvis snarled. Regis didn't move. "Yesterday you said your life had turned around, and today it's like nothing happened. So you got ghosts! We all got ghosts, Regis! You got LeRoy, I got Jesse Garon and then some. But you've turned yours into a stinking alibi! An alibi for being a loser and giving up on your God-given chance to love a good woman with one pure heart!"

"Leave me alone, Elvis."

"Hell I will!" Elvis snapped back. "We started this thing together and we're going to finish it together. Now put your head under the spigot and let's get to work."

"What work? Squirm is—"

"He ain't dead yet. At least far as I know. Wash your ugly face, Regis. Sober up, man!"

Elvis picked up the phone, dialed the operator, and told her to get him the number for the *Los Angeles Times*. Seconds later, he was put through to Mike Murphy at the city desk.

"Mr. Murphy, this is Elvis Presley."

"Sure, buddy. And I'm Frank Sinatra." A pause and Elvis heard Murphy's muffled voice call out to his office mates, "Got another 'Missing Elvis!' Number three this morning!"

"Listen, Mr. Murphy, I made your acquaintance the other day at a press conference over at MGM. You're the one asked me to comment on something Hal Wallis told you. Something not too flattering, as I recall."

"Jesus, you *are* Elvis, aren't you?"

"Through and through," Elvis said. "We don't have much time, Murphy, so listen up. I've got reason to believe Squirm Littlejon's escape is no accident. It's a set-up so the authorities can hunt him down. Hunt him down and kill him."

"Jesus!"

"Murphy, you got to get this out fast so they don't dare do it. So folks will get riled up real bad if they even try. It can't wait for tomorrow's paper. Can you do that?"

"I can put it out on the wire. They'd pick it up on radio in less than an hour," Murphy said. "But, Elvis, I need more. A lot more. Like who the hell set this thing up? And I need to know for sure that it's really you. I can't run with a story like this without—"

"It's me, all right, and time's running out. The troopers could have Littlejon in their sights already."

"If this is a hoax, I'll lose my job, damnit."

"Your *job*, Murphy! Not your *life!*"

"Where are you, Elvis?"

"West Hollywood," Elvis said. "I'll tell you exactly where if you promise to put that story on the wire right now. *Immediately!* Then you can get yourself over here and I'll give you more. An exclusive." A long pause at the other end. Then, "Deal. Where are you Elvis?" Elvis gave him Regis's address. "I'll be here for an hour, no longer," he told the reporter and hung up.

Regis was back standing behind his desk, water streaming down his face onto his jacket. He looked halfway to sober.

"Get me Dr. Garcia on the phone," Elvis barked at him.

Regis snapped to the task like an army recruit. He handed Elvis the phone while it was ringing at the other end. Delores Suarez picked up in Santa Teresa.

"Buenos tardes."

"Dr. Suarez, this is Elvis. I'm back in California with Regis and I got to talk with Dr. Garcia, ma'am. Is he there?"

Garcia came on the line a moment later.

"Hector, we got an emergency going up here. Littlejon's escaped and they're hunting him with rifles. We've gotta move fast. Can you get yourself up here right away? I'll pay for everything, of course."

"This is very sudden."

"I know it is, Doctor. First, I couldn't wait forty years. Now I can't wait a day."

Garcia hesitated for only a moment. "I will make arrangements immediately, Mr. Presley," he said.

"Thank you, Doctor," Elvis said. "Bring what you can for that DNA fingerprinting. I'll fix you up with a lab up here for the rest."

"Very good."

"And Doctor?"

"Yes, Mr. Presley?"

"Bring Dr. Suarez with you, if you don't mind. We need all the help we can get."

"I will see if that can be arranged," Garcia said.

Elvis told him to call back with his arrival time. When he hung up, Regis was still standing in front of him, still dripping, but now looking extremely agitated.

"I . . . I'm not sure I'm ready to see Delores just yet," he stammered.

"Then don't look at her," Elvis snapped. "Now what about Holly's safety deposit box? I want to get in there today."

"Not possible," Regis said. "I looked into it. You need to petition the court to appoint a personal representative for the estate. And before you even do that you have to conduct a search to make sure there's no existing trustee or conservatoire. And then you've got to wait until they set a hearing date for—"

"Hold on, Regis. If I walked into the bank today with the key to Holly's deposit box and said I wanted to get into it, what would they ask me for?"

"That's what I'm telling you. They'd need a court order designating you as the personal representative of the estate."

"What does it look like?"

"What?"

"That court order thing. What does it look like?"

"You know, it's an official document of the State of California," Regis said. "Letterhead, official seal, judge's signature."

"You got one of those?"

"You mean from another case? Yes, somewhere, I suppose." Regis gestured toward his file cabinets.

"Get it!" Elvis snapped. "Then get your friend next door to make up a new one for Holly's estate with me as trustee or whatever the heck it is. If he can do passports, this should be a piece of cake."

"I could be disbarred for—"

"*Disbarred?* From what—the corner saloon? Get it, Regis! Get moving now!"

Once again, Regis hopped to it like a buck private.

Elvis picked up the phone again and had the long-distance operator connect him with Bob Reardon's private line at CCI.

"Warden Reardon here," a decidedly tired and taut voice said. "It's me, Elvis."

"Jesus, Elvis! I can't talk with you now!"

"Reardon, don't shoot him, you hear? Order your men—"

"Right, heard all about it on the radio," Reardon groaned. "You don't know what the hell you're talking about, buddy."

"You're a patsy, Reardon. They're using you. After they're done, they'll hang you up to dry."

"Go to hell, Elvis!" Reardon blurted. "I've got enough grief without you—"

"Don't shoot him, you hear?"

The phone went dead. Elvis tapped the cradle until he got the operator again. This time he gave her the number for the William Jackson Clinic in Alamo. While it rang, Elvis watched Regis pull a file out of a cabinet and start for the door.

"It's out on the radio already," Elvis called to him. "That should make them think twice about pulling any triggers out in Tehachapi."

"Let's hope so," Regis said. He actually saluted Elvis before heading next door to the Rodriguez Travel and Counterfeiting Agency.

The receptionist put Elvis right through to Billy Jackson.

"What's happening, Mr. P?"

"More than I can tell you right now, Billy. But listen, are you still in contact with Connie Spinelli?"

"*Close* contact," Billy said. There was a smile in his voice.

"How close?"

"She's staying with me here in Alamo. I've been meaning to call you and tell you all about, but things have been moving kind of fast in my life, friend."

"I'm real glad for you, Billy. But I want you to keep a close eye on Miss Spinelli. I'm dealing with some awful people out here. Terrible people. And they seem to have one heck of a long reach."

"I hear you, I'll look after her," Billy said. "Listen, you want to say hello to her? Actually, she's been meaning to call you herself."

"Sure."

Connie Spinelli came on with a girlish, "Hi there, Mr. Presley."

"You sure sound good, Miss Spinelli."

"Never been happier," she replied. "Listen, Elvis, I happened to think of something the other day. I don't think it means anything, but remember when I said the man who threatened me had a World War One army outfit on? Looked all spick-and-span like it wasn't real, but out of a studio wardrobe?"

"Yes, I remember that."

"Well, the thing I remembered is that one time my friend Patty over in wardrobe told me that this exec kept borrowing outfits from her. Mostly World War One stuff. All the same size. And Patty said she knew it couldn't be for a movie, because they weren't shooting any war pictures at the time."

"What was his name?" Elvis asked. "The executive, I mean."

"It was a she," Miss Spinelli replied. "Woman named Aronson over in development."

"Thank you, Connie," Elvis said.

"I'll put Billy back on," she said.

"Mr. P.?" Billy's voice.

"What is it, friend?"

"You take care, you hear? I can't be losing any more kin in this lifetime."

"God bless, Billy."

"God bless, Mr. P."

As soon as Elvis got the dial tone again, he called the Colonel's office at MGM without so much as taking a breath.

"Parker here."

"Tom, it's me. Any calls?"

A sound like a sputtering lawnmower erupted in Elvis's ear. For the first time that morning, Elvis had to smile.

"Any calls?" Parker bellowed. "Any *calls*? Nothing *but* calls, nonstop. *New York Times*. ABC radio. *Where are you?* What the hell are *you* up to, Elvis?"

"Taking care of business," Elvis said.

"*Whose* bloody business, boy?"

"Squirm Littlejon's, for one."

"Jesus, Elvis! You're killing us, do you know that? Killing every damned thing I ever worked for. They're going crazy over here. The last thing MGM wants is for this Littlejon business to burst into some kind of—"

"I don't give a mare's rear end what MGM wants, Colonel," Elvis hissed.

"By God, you will, son!" Parker barked back. "You will and then it's going to be too late. You got a demon inside you, boy. A demon that's doing it's damnedest to destroy you."

"I got a demon, all right, Colonel," Elvis replied evenly. "And he's been suffocating for years."

Elvis hung up before Parker could say another word. Regis was back, standing in front of him with a surprisingly animated expression on his face. He'd probably snuck in another little tequila toast with his friend, Rodriguez. Never mind—at least he was back in action again.

"Rodriguez'll have that court order made up in a couple of hours," Regis reported proudly. "I got inspired in there, Elvis. Listen to this." He unfolded a piece of paper and read, "'This instrument grants access, including but not limited to, the following sites and institutions: Barclay's Bank of London, Los Angeles Savings and Loan, the Brink's Bank,—'See that? I bury it in there so they'll never suspect—"

"You're a genius, Regis," Elvis said, rising. "But it's time to pack up, partner. Grab that DNA kit. We're going to a funeral."

18

THE CEREMONIAL BLOTTING OF THE TEARS

MIKE Murphy was coming up the stairs two steps at a time as Elvis and Regis came scrambling down. Murphy was a lanky young man with a freckled face that didn't quite fit with his prematurely bald head.

"Mr. Presley! Thank God, it *is* you."

"Mr. Murphy, glad you could make it," Elvis said, not missing a step. "I do appreciate you keeping your end of our bargain. Word's out on the radio, I hear."

Murphy made an abrupt about-face on the stairs and fell in step behind them.

"My ass is really on the line, you know, Elvis," Murphy said.

"Whose isn't these days?" Regis chimed. The man's mouth was clearly in full working order again.

Grabbing one of his crutches from the wall on his way out the door, Elvis used it as a cane as he made his way to his car. Murphy followed and automatically got into the back seat when Elvis opened the door for him. Regis gave directions to the L.A. suburb of Maywood and they were on their way.

Elvis snapped on the car radio and scanned up and down the dial, stopping whenever he heard an announcer's voice. In five minutes time, they heard three separate news bulletins on Elvis Presley's suspicions about the Littlejon prison escape. Two of the three included droll allusions to the questionable status of Elvis's mental condition, one of these suggesting that he was popping pills of some kind, but Elvis couldn't have cared less because all three reports concluded with an update on the manhunt in the Tehachapi Mountains: Not a sign of Frederick Littlejon. The Squirm slithered on.

Elvis gave Murphy a run-down on what he'd been up to the last few days, leaving out parts and names that he didn't want in the press just yet—no mention of Connie Spinelli, nothing about Holly McDougal's call-girl operation or her impressive savings account. But he went into detail about Garcia's conclusive medical evidence that someone other than Squirm Littlejon had had sex with Holly just prior to her murder.

"Let me get this straight, Presley," Murphy intoned from the back seat after Elvis had finished. "This stuntman, Grieves, was probably threatening you, but you're not absolutely sure. And he may have been responsible for Will Cathcart's death, but it might have just been some crazy bull with high blood pressure. But the one thing you are sure of is that this doctor somewhere in the middle of Mexico has figured out a way to pin-point who exactly had sexual intercourse with who and when. Except that nobody in the world believes him."

"That's right," Elvis replied.

"I better start looking for work immediately," Murphy groaned.

"I got a job for you already," Elvis said.

There was only one Christian cemetery in Maywood but by the time they found it, the funeral service was already in progress. Elvis opened up the cell-gathering kit that Dr. Garcia had put together for him. He made up vials with a few drops of suspensory fluid in the bottom, pasted blank labels to each, then handed Regis a handful of tweezers, eyedroppers, and little squares of blotting paper, and stashed the rest in his jacket pocket.

"Garcia says just about anything does the trick," Elvis said. "A fleck of skin, a teardrop, a strand of hair. They all got the same markers under a microscope."

Murphy rolled his eyes heavenward; he looked like a man who had just gotten off the plane in the wrong country.

"Got to be sure you got the right name with the right sample, otherwise it's useless," Elvis went on. "That's your job, Murphy. Maybe tell them you're doing a story on the funeral for the *Times* and you want to spell their names right."

"Just like that," Murphy said incredulously. "While they're saying the Lord's Prayer, you and Regis attack them with eyedroppers, and then I ask them to spell their names."

"Something like that," Elvis said, pulling out his crutch from behind the driver's seat. "We'll play it by ear."

Indeed, the preacher *was* leading the assembled mourners in the Lord's Prayer as Elvis, Regis, and Murphy approached the grave site. As Elvis had hoped, there was a load of the stuntmen present—he recognized some of them from pictures he'd been in, and the rest he could tell by their bowed legs and leathery faces. Squirm's fellow stuntmen were surely prime suspects. There was no sign of Grieves, though, and that was a real disappointment because he was at the top of his suspect list.

There were several surprising mourners on hand: Miss Aronson was standing next to Ned Florbid, MGM's production executive, both in expensive-looking tailored black outfits. Pretty high level representation from the studio for the funeral of a stuntman— especially for one who'd only been working for them for a year. And, lo and behold, standing just behind Jilly-Jo Cathcart and her two children was none other than Wayne LeFevre. Now what the devil was *he* doing here? Whatever the reason, Elvis was glad he was here; ever since Elvis had heard Wayne's oily encouragements on Holly's bump-and-grind screen test, he had suspected that his double had developed more than a passing acquaintanceship with the murdered teenager. This little stop at the Maywood Cemetery held the promise of being unusually efficient.

They were up to "Give us this day our daily bread" when the first mourner spotted Elvis limping toward the grave. She was a frail-looking woman of about forty in what was undoubtedly her Sunday dress and probably had been for a couple decades of Sundays. A neighbor or rodeo wife, Elvis figured. When she saw Elvis, she stopped in mid-prayer and crossed herself like she had just had a vision of the Holy Mother. She nudged the woman next to her, pointed with her eyes, and when this other woman saw Elvis, she stopped praying too, right before she'd been forgiven her trespasses. Then a third mourner spotted Elvis and only few seconds later the preacher was left to finish the Lord's Prayer on his own, Amen.

Total silence as everyone stared at Elvis and his companions. The color came up in Ned Florbid's face so fast that he looked like he had acquired an instant sunburn. Miss Aronson winked nervously at Elvis. And Wayne LeFevre did a double take worthy of Buster Keaton.

"Forgive me for coming so late, Miss Jilly-Jo," Elvis said finally, nodding to the widow.

"Honored you could make it at all, Elvis," Jilly-Jo responded, nodding back to him.

The preacher, a white-haired, bushy-eyebrowed man in black clerical robes, gave Elvis a flinty stare which said that in the eyes of the Lord, Elvis was just another sinner. Elvis had to agree with that, all right, especially considering what his mission was on this sacred ground.

"Going to sing the hymn for us, Mr. Presley?" It was the poor-looking woman who had first spotted him.

"If that's what Miss Jilly-Jo and the preacher desire," Elvis replied softly.

Jilly-Jo looked expectantly at the clergyman who sighed and then said grudgingly, "I guess that would be all right."

Quickly, Elvis dug into his pocket and slipped Regis his share of the cell-gathering kit. "Go for the teardrops," he whispered urgently. He closed his eyes and offered up a silent prayer, begging the Lord's forgiveness for the duplicity in what he was about to do, and then he spread his arms wide and began to sing:

> *On the other side of Jordan*
> *Where the tree of life is blooming*
> *There is rest for the weary*
> *There is rest for me . . .*

It was Elvis's favorite gospel hymn, full of comfort and redemption, and loaded, too, with memories of that funeral at the colored church in Maury City where he'd first met Billy Jackson. There was no problem singing it pure and from the heart—there never was. But as he sang, and as he watched the soulful strains work their way into even the most hardened hearts of those assembled at Will Cathcart's grave, Elvis felt a hollowness deep in his soul. If it was a sin to sing a bloodless song in a Hollywood movie, it was surely a worse sin to sing a masterpiece of feeling for the sole purpose of turning heartfelt tears into incriminating evidence.

But that is exactly what he was doing and, by God, it was working. Everyone was now weeping, including LeFevre, even if he was well known for his playacting. Didn't matter—tears were tears however you produced them.

Through half-opened eyes, Elvis watched as Regis and Murphy approached the woman who had first spotted him. Regis handed her a square of blotting paper like it was some kind of holy sacrament. She hesitated, looking inquiringly at Elvis. Elvis gave her a solemn nod, like a personal benediction, and she took the paper, dabbed her tears, and returned it to Regis's outstretched hand. Murphy moved in to get her whispered name, jotted it down on a page of his reporter's notebook, then pressed the little square of tear-damp blotting paper under the name and flipped the page as Regis approached the next mourner. Smooth as silk, like a pair of altar boys who'd been doing this their whole lives.

It was as if he had created a brand new ritual—*the ceremonial blotting of the tears*—and the folks just accepted it as part of the service. Well, heck, how did any ritual get its start anyway? The wafers and wine, the holy water, the memorial candles? Somebody had to get it going the first time, somebody the congregation trusted to know the right and proper thing to do. Somebody they *venerated*, like Elvis Presley, the King.

O Lord, it is a fearsome power and I am unworthy of it.

Regis and Murphy kept passing among the mourners, offering up the little squares of blotting paper to mop their tears and then taking them back. Not to be left out, the preacher himself reached for one of the squares, dabbed his tears, and then, going one better, gave the ritual his personal imprimatur by pressing the blotting paper to his lips before returning it to Regis. Florbid was next, dutifully following the preacher's example—he was, after all, a company man. But when Murphy approach little Miss Aronson in her Rodeo Drive-mourning suit, the two eyed one another suspiciously before getting on with the ceremonial blotting.

Wayne LeFevre was another story. He smelled a rat and started to back away from the open grave the moment he saw Regis begin his little operation. No ceremonial blotting of the tears for Wayne, especially not with Squirm Littlejon's attorney as the altar boy. Elvis caught Murphy's eye and gestured toward LeFevre.

> *There is rest for the weary*
> *There is rest for the weary*

Elvis repeated the chorus as Murphy strode rapidly toward the retreating LeFevre. Elvis's double spun around and broke into a trot with Murphy now jogging behind him.

> *There is rest for the weary*
> *There is rest for the weary*

Elvis raised both hands, palms out, a regular preacher man blessing his flock as he watched Murphy closing in, his right arm outstretched. He was pointing his tweezers at LeFevre like it was a lethal weapon.

> *There is rest for the weary*
> *There is rest for the weary*

Murphy's hand shot out to the back of LeFevre's head, the tweezers gleaming in the midday sun. Suddenly, his hand snapped back and he came to a halt. He raised his tweezers high and grinned at Elvis. Cell specimen No. 16: a strand of Wayne LeFevre's hair! Wayne yelped a few choice words unbefitting these hallowed grounds and darted across the street.

> *There is rest for me.*

Elvis brought the hymn to a close and the minister immediately handed a shovel to Jilly-Jo to throw the first soil on her husband's coffin. Next came her children, and now Elvis fell in line with the rest to take his turn. Ned Florbid and the Aronson woman managed to squeeze in just behind him.

"That was beautiful, Elvis," Aronson whispered, touching Elvis's sleeve. "Very poignant. Very James Dean. I kept seeing the last scene in *Rebel Without a Cause*. Something for us to think about, eh?"

Elvis starred at her incredulously.

"Good to see you, Elvis," Florbid was saying. "I didn't realize Cathcart's a friend of yours."

"Was," Elvis murmured. "Strange Mickey Grieves isn't here. He was a good friend too, wasn't he?"

"He's working today. Monster picture," Florbid said, then went on quickly, "We really have to talk, Elvis. Maybe we can grab lunch together after this."

Elvis followed the line a step forward, not responding to Florbid.

"We all want the same thing, you know," Florbid pressed on. "I mean, the studio is a hundred percent behind you on this Littlejon business. But there must be some way of handling it without causing so much—"

"Please!" Elvis hissed, craning his head down so that his face was just a couple of inches from Florbid's. "A little respect. We're at a *funeral*, for heaven's sake!"

Later, when they were back on the road, Regis and Murphy in the back seat stuffing little squares of damp blotting paper into the liquid in the test vials and inscribing the labels with their donors' names, Murphy asked Elvis who the little bleached-blond woman was. Elvis told him that it was Nancy Pollard's assistant, Aronson. "Why'd you ask?"

"Thought I'd seen her before, but probably not," Murphy said. "She's just a type, Hollywood standard issue."

Elvis then related his encounter with Florbid. When he got to the part where he said, "A little respect. We're at a funeral, for heaven's sake!" all three started to laugh so hard that Elvis had to pull over to the shoulder and wait until they finished lest they spill their precious cargo of tears.

19
ELVIS'S PERSONAL BIOGRAPHER

THE latest news out of Tehachapi was not good at all. Dogs had picked up Squirm's scent in the northeast corner of the mountain range, and now there was talk of bringing in National Guard helicopters, although Governor Brown hadn't signed off on that yet. The story of Elvis's claim that the whole thing was a set-up so they could shoot Littlejon had completely evaporated from the airwaves.

"A story like that doesn't have much staying power," Mike Murphy explained from the back seat. "If they repeat it too much, it just sounds crazy."

"We need a new story then," Elvis said, turning onto the West Hollywood exit. "Something else to make them think twice before they go ahead and shoot Squirm. Probably shouldn't have my name attached to it this time, you think? I'm getting the reputation as an unreliable source, as you folks say."

"Can't help you there, Elvis," Murphy said. "You can't just make something up and put it on the news, you know."

"Why not?" Regis chortled. "Half the stuff you hear on the news is the figment of *somebody's* imagination. Usually some politician's." Elvis hung a right onto Sunset Boulevard.

"How about something about the FBI coming up with a new suspect in the McDougal murder?" Elvis suddenly said excitedly. "Hot on his trail and all. That might do it. What do you think?"

"I think I'd better get back to my office and see if I still have a job," Murphy said soberly.

"I'm serious, Murphy, that's not bad, right? Folks respect the FBI."

"Forget it, Elvis," Murphy said.

"You can use the old 'anonymous sources' bit," Regis piped up. "Fits perfectly. Everybody knows the FBI is ultra secretive."

"He's right," Elvis said. "Your paper had that anonymous source's fella telling stories about me only yesterday."

"Let me out at the next corner, Elvis," Murphy said resolutely. "I've paid my dues to you already, thank you."

"You sure have, Mr. Murphy," Elvis said. "Especially over there in Maywood. Man, you've got the fastest tweezers in the West." Murphy had to laugh in spite of himself.

"I'm sorry, Elvis," he said. "This has been terrific. A day to tell my grandchildren about. But I'm a journalist and we have an ethical code."

"Yup, that ethical code had me holed up in a hotel room in London with Ann-Margret just last night," Elvis said.

"Can't do it, Elvis," Murphy said. "Sorry."

They drove in silence for a few moments before Elvis said quietly, "I've been thinking of doing my biography, you know? My life as I see it. I'd need a writer, of course."

For several minutes no one said anything. Then Murphy burst out with, "Jesus, Elvis! You drive one hell of bargain!"

"I just happen to like you, Murphy," Elvis replied, grinning. "Now how about that? There's a phone booth right on the corner there." He pulled the Eldorado up to the curb right beside a phone booth. He looked in the rearview mirror: in the back seat, Mike Murphy was kneading his long forehead, a look of panic on his freckled face. "I'm engaged," Murphy mumbled. "Getting married next month."

"Congratulations," Elvis said. "She'll be real proud of you. You're doing the right thing."

Regis leaned across Murphy and pushed open the car door.

"Do I get my name on the cover?" Murphy asked.

"In blue suede," Elvis said. "Bigger than mine if you like."

Murphy got out and entered the phone booth, leaving the door to it partially open. Elvis rolled down all the car windows and listened. Murphy had to give some kind of code word proving his identify to the editor on the other end, then launched into his story about the anonymous source who confirmed that the FBI had a new suspect in the McDougal murder case. Apparently the editor was more than a little skeptical.

"Can't give you his name, Doug," Murphy was saying. "Protected source. The guy could lose his job, you know."

Pause.

"No, it's not Littlejon. They're clear on that."

Pause.

"They won't say, Doug. Don't want to tip him off that they're hot on his trail. They shouldn't have told me as much as they did, believe me."

Pause.

"A bulletin, right. On the wire immediately."

Pause.

"You bet, Doug. As soon as I hear anything else."

Murphy hung up. He remained in the booth for several seconds, then came stumbling out to the curb where he bent over and spewed up his breakfast. Poor devil. Truth to tell, it was kind of reassuring to see that some people still got sick when they told a lie. Elvis sure wouldn't have guessed Murphy to be one of them. Murphy probably really was a good choice for his biographer.

"You done good," Elvis said when Murphy got back into the car.

"I bet you could use a drink," Regis said, producing his flask, but Murphy waved it off. Elvis scowled at Regis in the mirror and Regis put away the flask without a nip.

"Let's say you're right," Murphy said seriously as Elvis started up the car again. "Let's say Littlejon is innocent, like your Spanish doctor insists. And let's say his escape really is a set-up so they can shoot him. If all that's true, we aren't just up against some stuntman, Elvis. It's got to be bigger than that. Mickey Grieves can lie on the stand and string you up in the stunt shack, but he can't pull strings in the California prison system. No way in hell Grieves can do that. He may be a cog in it, just like Warden Reardon, but he's not running the machine."

"I'm thinking the same thing," Elvis said. "But that's where I get stuck. Who's got that kind of pull?"

"Politicians and movie stars," Regis said. "People like you."

"Baloney," Elvis said. "You don't think I could've called up Reardon and told him to turn Littlejon loose, do you?"

"Maybe," Regis said. "If he thought that would get 'The Singing Warden' into production, I can see him doing something like that."

"Never," Elvis said.

"Don't underestimate yourself, Elvis," Murphy said. "I'm here to tell you that you're one hell of persuasive man."

Elvis laughed.

"Guess I could've saved a whole lot of trouble if that's what I'd done in the first place," he said. "Had Reardon turn Littlejon loose, but nobody following him with a rifle. Heck, making the warden's fool movie picture would've been worth it. Probably no worse than the movies I been making."

"You mind if I take notes?" Murphy piped from the back seat, pulling out his notepad.

"Go right ahead," Elvis said. "Put that in our book. I can't stand my movies, not a one of them since *Wild in the Country*. Truth is, I wouldn't put down a wooden nickel to see any of them myself."

"You're kidding me," Murphy said, scratching away in his pad.

"Hey, would I kid my personal biographer?" Elvis said.

All three of them started to laugh again. Man, it felt good, it felt right. Riding along in a car with a couple of buddies, speaking the honest truth to each other while pulling the wool over everybody else's eyes. It felt like the old days, tooting around Tennessee with Scotty and Bill, playing little clubs and waiting for the future to happen. *Just being yourself.*

By the time they pulled up in front of Regis's office on West Eighth Street, the first bulletin had already hit the air: anonymous source, FBI suspect, Littlejon's innocence—the whole ball of wax. When it came on the radio, Mike Murphy said he felt sick again, but this time he managed to keep all remaining cookies down.

Rodriguez was waiting for them at the top of the stairs holding up his freshly minted court order complete with letterhead, California state seal, and judge's elaborate signature.

"A masterpiece," Rodriguez announced. "It is the best work I ever do."

Murphy leaned over, peering at the document which designated Elvis Presley as the personal representative of Holly McDougal's estate.

"Holy Mother," Murphy murmured. "I'm in with a den of criminals."

Elvis handed Rodriguez a hundred dollars in twenties, shook his hand, and took the court order.

"Bank closes at two thirty. We don't have much time," he said. He told Murphy to stash the tear vials and Wayne's hair sample in Rodriguez's refrigerator, then told Regis to get ahold of Holly's sister and have her meet them immediately at the Los Angeles Savings and Loan with Holly's safety deposit box key. They were back in the car in five minutes flat.

Mike Murphy had certainly earned his right to hear what Elvis had omitted from his original story, so Elvis and Regis filled him in on Holly McDougal's private call-girl operation on the MGM lot, along with the stunning total of her late life's savings.

"It's undoubtedly one of her johns who murdered her," Murphy announced from the back seat after they had finished.

"What makes you say that?" Elvis asked.

"I must have covered a dozen call-girl murders when I was on the city desk," Murphy replied. "And nine times out of ten, it's either her pimp or one of her johns who did it. Well, it sounds like Miss McDougal was self-employed—no pimp—so that leaves her customers. And by the way, that doesn't eliminate our friend Littlejon. He may not have been a paying customer, but he was still a john."

"Why?" Elvis asked. "Why do they do it?"

"Craziness," Murphy said. "Fits of disgust. They hate themselves for sinking so low, and they turn it around and blame it on the whore. *She's* the Jezebel. *She's* the one who made them sin, so she has to be punished."

"Dr. Freud again," Regis said.

"Sometimes it's another kind of craziness," Murphy went on. "Humiliation. Sexual humiliation. Say the john can't get it up or he's self-conscious about his size or something like that. The girl smiles at him funny, probably not meaning anything at all by it, but the john gets it in his head that she's laughing at him and goes berserk. Strangles her in a rage."

Elvis shook his head. In the past few days he'd heard enough about sexual craziness—especially of the male variety—to last him a lifetime.

"We're closing in, friends," Regis said gleefully. "Process of elimination. He was one of Holly's customers *and* he has a lot of power. Enough power to get Reardon to do his bidding. And to get Will Cathcart offed by a bull."

"*If*," Murphy said. "*If* any one of your cockamamie assumptions is true. Especially that one about the raging bull that's a hit man."

Elvis glanced at Murphy in the rearview mirror. He had the panicked look of a man being strangled by second thoughts.

"I'm sorry, gentleman," Murphy said quietly. "But it still makes more sense to me that Littlejon is McDougal's murderer *and* he's a talented escape artist. Occam's Razor—the simplest explanation is usually the right one."

"*Damnation!* It's him again!" Elvis hollered.

The baby blue Beetle had suddenly appeared in his mirror, swinging directly in back of him from the right lane. Same driver in the same nightwatch cap, but this time Elvis got a better look at what the man was waving in his hand: a cardboard box with a gleaming, blood-red skull and crossbones painted on its cover. Elvis floored the accelerator and the Eldorado lurched forward, its tires spitting sparks.

"What the hell?" Murphy sputtered as he was thrown back against his seat.

Next to Elvis, Regis had pivoted around and was staring out the rear window.

"Mean-looking bastard!" he cheered. "Man's been threatening Elvis ever since he got on this case. Got a simple explanation for that, Murphy?"

Elvis was weaving in and out of traffic at sixty-plus, but every time he looked in the mirror he saw the Beetle still hanging on his tail.

"Must have a Corvette engine in that darn thing!" Elvis called, hanging a hard right and cutting across two lanes onto the shoulder where he kept the pedal floored, bouncing from one pothole to the next as he shot past the cars on his left.

"Hell, let him catch us, Elvis!" Regis crowed. He was clearly having the time of his life. "There's three of us. We can take him."

"No, *please*," Murphy moaned. He had crawled down into the space behind the driver's seat and was trembling. "Really. He could have a gun."

"No problem!" Regis cackled. "He'll only have time to shoot one of us."

Elvis took the first exit on two wheels, flashed through the red light where the exit lane met the access road, made a U-turn, and tore back onto the highway. His timing was perfect. Six cars ahead of them was the Beetle. Elvis had not only lost their pursuer, he was now behind him.

"Whoopee!" Elvis howled.

"Gorgeous!" Regis cheered. "Work of art, Elvis!"

Murphy's shiny pate emerged from behind Elvis. His face was flushed but he was grinning from ear to ear. He raised his right hand in a flourishing salute and cried out, *"Athos!"*

"Aramis!" Regis chimed in, also raising his right hand.

Elvis looked over at Regis questioningly.

"Say, 'Porthos,'" Regis murmured.

"What for?"

"The Three Musketeers," Regis said. "He's the third."

Elvis nodded. He was quiet for a moment, then slowly released his right hand from the steering wheel and held it aloft. "Porthos," he mumbled.

Both Regis and Murphy immediately began thumping Elvis on his shoulders, laughing and cheering and bouncing in their seats. Yup, it was just like the old days tooting around Tennessee with Scotty and Will, even if half the time he didn't know what the heck Murphy and Regis were talking about.

As they approached the East L.A. branch of the Savings and Loan bank, Regis pointed out Norma McDougal waiting for them. Norma was still wearing her pea green smock for bed-pan duty at the nursing home where she worked, but even in a Dior gown she wouldn't have looked like much. Funny thing was, she definitely looked like a sister to Holly—blond hair, turned-up nose, saucer eyes—but every feature was just a tad off, a fraction too much. The blond hair looked like soiled sand instead of new-grown wheat, the up-turned nose bordered on the piggy, and Norma's saucer eyes were so wide set that the one on the left looked like a walleye. The line between beauty and beast was a narrow one, all right. Probably if you looked at their DNA side by side under Dr. Garcia's microscope, there wouldn't be a whole of difference between Norma's and Holly's—just a microscopic speck that made all the difference in the world.

But what was that difference, really? Norma McDougal may have been the beauty-deprived sister, but she was surely the only living one. And standing in front of the Savings and Loan in her spattered smock, she had a look of childlike hopefulness on her homely face—probably evoked by the prospect of coming into her late sister's savings account, a small fortune that would allow her to throw away that smock forever. But whatever put that expression there, it was surely a look of living and breathing hope.

When Norma saw Elvis Presley exit the car along with Regis and Murphy, that look changed to stupefaction, then to near ecstasy. She backed up unsteadily against the bank window, blushing deeply.

"Afternoon, ma'am," Elvis said, extending his hand. "Glad you could make it so quick."

Norma stared at him, speechless. She couldn't quite get her hand out to meet his.

"Got the key?" Regis asked.

Norma nodded, and then Elvis led the way, limping without his crutch into the local branch of Los Angeles Savings and Loan.

It was one of those frozen-action things again, like a single film frame locked on the Moviola screen. The entire bank—customers, tellers, officers, security men—came to an abrupt halt, whatever they were doing, and gaped at Elvis.

"Good afternoon," Elvis said to one and all.

"Good afternoon, Elvis," one and all replied in chorus.

One of the bank officers came surging forward, trying to assume a just-another-day-at-the-office expression on his baby face.

"How may I help you, Mr. Presley?" he said.

Elvis pulled the spanking new court order from his pocket and unfurled it in front of the banker's face.

"Need to get into the safety box of Miss Holly McDougal," Elvis announced. "This here gives me permission to—"

The bank officer led the way to the vault without so much as a glance at the document; apparently, it was not good form to question the documentation of such an important new customer. Rodriguez would be disappointed to hear that his outstanding work had gone unappreciated.

"These people are with you, I assume," the banker said, gesturing to Elvis's entourage as they waited for a guard to open the barred gate to the vault.

"They surely are," Elvis replied. "This here is my lawyer, Mr. Regis Clifford. And this is Miss Norma McDougal, Miss Holly's sister. And over there is Mr. Michael Murphy. He's my personal biographer, writes down every little thing I do."

"A pleasure," the banker said. His nothing special going on here demeanor was rapidly being replaced by an expression of golly a celebrity close enough to touch. Elvis wished the man had stuck with his first attitude.

Norma slipped Elvis the key, then he and the banker entered the vault where the banker inserted the master key into one slot and showed Elvis where to insert his. Elvis slid out Holly McDougal's safety deposit box. It was heavy and awkward to carry, its contents rattling and shifting as Elvis limped out of the vault behind the banker. A horseshoe of gawkers had assembled just outside the barred gate to the vault and now the banker hissed for them to give Elvis some privacy, like a zookeeper shielding his prize bear at feeding time. Elvis, Regis, Murphy, and Norma followed the banker into a little cubicle where Elvis set the box on a counter and then let himself down heavily into the sole chair. Darned ankle was acting up again. Elvis lifted the box's hinged cover.

Its contents glistened like a galaxy of stars. There were enough diamond and emerald bracelets and necklaces to deck out an entire royal family.

"Jesus!" Murphy said, Regis echoing him a beat behind.

"Hot dog!" Norma McDougal exclaimed. At this point in her mind she probably wasn't simply jettisoning her nursing-home smock, she was replacing it with gowns from every shop on Rodeo Drive. "Where the heck did Holly get this stuff?"

"Good question," Elvis said. Although Norma might be pleased to hear that her beautiful, angelic sister had been into prostitution, Elvis didn't see any reason to tell her—not yet, at least. In any event, this display of gems confirmed his suspicion that Holly must have been involved in a more profitable enterprise than simply charging rent for her young body.

Regis abruptly reached for the one necklace that was all diamonds, brought it close to his face and studied it.

"You know something about jewelry?" Elvis asked him.

"Not really," Regis said, setting the necklace back into the box. "My mother had a weakness for diamonds that my good father indulged. But she never wore them outside the house. Afraid they'd get stolen. Kept them in a safe, just like Holly."

"Don't see the sense in that," Elvis said.

"Simple greed," Murphy said. "Like those people who buy stolen Rembrandts on the black market. They can't show them to anyone, but late at night they take them out, gaze at them and think, 'That's mine. All mine.'"

"Still don't see the sense," Elvis said, poking at one of the bracelets. He wondered vaguely what Priscilla would do if he brought something like it home to her. Wear it to the drive-in?

"First thing to do is figure out if any of it is stolen," Regis said. "And probably best not to involve the authorities."

Norma looked aghast. Surely it wasn't the possibility that her late sister had been a thief that bothered her. No, it was the chance that some of this treasure would have to be returned to its rightful owner.

"I know a jeweler who keeps up on stolen items," Murphy said. "He's been known to keep a secret too."

"Give him a call," Elvis said. "And see how fast he can get over here."

They all had to wait while Norma did a thorough inventory of the jewelry, describing each piece in meticulous detail in a notebook she had brought along—the girl was nothing if not efficient. Then Elvis returned the box to the vault. Back at the banker's desk, Murphy phoned his jeweler friend while Elvis signed several documents giving the jeweler permission to inspect Holly's treasure trove on the premises. Elvis also signed several sheets of the banker's personal stationery, autographs for every member of his family plus a few favorite clients. In exchange, the banker promised to hang around after closing time with a security guard to let the jeweler in to do his business.

Outside, Elvis offered to give Norma a lift back to the nursing home, but she gave him a lopsided smile and said she'd rather walk, and that, anyway, she wasn't going back to the nursing home today or any other day. Man, she was spending her sister's money already; Elvis sure hoped she was legally entitled to it. In the meantime, he dug into his pocket, pulled out three fifty-dollar bills, and handed them to her.

"What's this for, Mr. Presley?" the girl asked, wide eyed.

"Lunch," Elvis said, getting into his car.

The FBI story was all over the car radio, already coupled with an adamant denial straight from J. Edgar Hoover's press secretary.

"Nice touch, that denial!" Regis cheered. "Now the story really sounds true!"

Murphy said that he was feeling nauseous again.

One of the radio reporters announced that Warden Reardon's dogs had just finished leading the search party in a futile four-mile arc in the northeast Tehachapi range, bringing it back to where they started from. He said there was talk of replacing both Reardon *and* his dogs. Elvis had to smile—he'd seen that one coming.

20
THE SHAME

REGIS's phone was ringing as the three men rambled into his office. Regis picked up; it was for Elvis.

"Elvis here."

"It's me, Binxter Bartley out in Sparks, Mr. Presley," the voice said. "Remember? I showed you the bull. Dead one."

"Yes, Mr. Bartley. I remember."

"I got Doc Freeman here," Bartley said. "The vet. I'm going to put him on, okay?"

"Sure thing."

"Mr. Presley? This Dr. Arthur Freeman." A high, twangy voice.

"Yes, Doctor."

"I can't tell you how strange this is," the vet said. "Talking to Mr. Elvis Presley in person."

"Yes, sir," Elvis said.

"Most of the time I just talk to animals, you know," Freeman went on. "Horses, cows, sheep. And here I am talking to Elvis Presley."

"Yes, Doctor, must be strange," Elvis said, sitting down behind Regis's desk.

"Can't get over it," Freeman said.

"Well, there you go," Elvis said. He was trying to bend over to massage his throbbing ankle, but couldn't quite reach it.

"So I looked at that bull what gored Cathcart," the veterinarian said. "Monster animal. Good ton of prime beef."

"Big," Elvis said encouragingly.

"So the deal is, somebody shot him up with Actrapid—pork insulin," Freeman said. "Enough to bring an elephant out of a diabetic coma."

"What?" Elvis sat upright again.

"I did a blood test on him," Freeman went on. "Looking for glucose. And it was off the charts. That's what made me test for insulin."

"You think that's what killed him?"

"The bull?"

"Cathcart."

"Both," the veterinarian said. "Animal was pumping so much sugar he was seeing red. Literally. Capillaries in his eyes must have been flooded. And that's just for starters. Blood pressure soaring, hormones going haywire. Any one of them is enough to make a bull go crazy *and* give him the strength of a whole team of oxen. At least for the five minutes or so before it makes his heart stop."

"You sure he was injected with it?" Elvis asked.

"Had to be," Freeman said. "You couldn't get a bull to eat that much pork insulin if you wrapped it in daisies."

"How soon before Cathcart climbed onto the bull would that have been?" Elvis asked.

"Couple of minutes," Freeman said. "No more than that or he'd of keeled over in the pen."

"Thank you, Doctor," Elvis said. "I'd sure appreciate it if you wrote all of this up and sent it to me." He gave him Regis's address. "Is Binxter still there?"

"Sure is, Mr. Presley," the vet said. "But before I sign off, I just got to tell you how much everyone out here in Sparks appreciates what you did yesterday. Righteous, you know? And funny how you dedicated that song to Squirm Littlejon, saying he was innocent and all, and now he's on the loose down there. It's like he heard you singing to him."

"Just a coincidence," Elvis said.

"Maybe," Freeman said. "But a funny coincidence anyways."

Binxter Bartley came on the line.

"Were you around the pen when Will got up on that bull?" Elvis asked him.

"Yup."

"Who else was there?"

"Joey," Bartley said. "He's the regular bull wrangler. Me and Tim—he's the other one helped you up on the bandstand. And then one of Will's pals from Hollywood."

"Mickey Grieves?"

"Yup, he was the one," Bartley said.

"Thank you, Binxter."

"My pleasure, Mr. Presley."

Elvis replaced the phone and looked up. Regis was on his way out the door to the hallway bathroom; Murphy was inspecting the lawyer's helter-skelter library.

"We got that one right," Elvis announced to Murphy. "Mickey Grieves killed Cathcart, even if he is just a cog in the machine. Get your tweezers out, Murph. We'll need a piece of his DNA before Garcia gets here."

While he was sitting at Regis's desk, Elvis made two more calls: one to his Bel Air doctor, Belizzi, who taught at U.C.L.A., and the other to the only hotel in the West Hollywood Yellow Pages that had a Spanish name, the San Vincente Inn. Belizzi reluctantly agreed to turn over a corner of his lab for a few days to Elvis's doctor friend from Mexico. And the receptionist at the San Vincente Inn said she would be delighted to reserve five of their very best rooms, starting tonight. The moment Elvis hung up on this second call, the phone rang again. He picked it up with, "Regis Clifford's law offices."

A man with what sounded like a German accent wanted to talk to Mike Murphy. He identified himself as a jeweler, and he said he was calling from an office at the Los Angeles Savings and Loan. Elvis waved Murphy over.

"Murphy here," was all Mike said and then he just listened, nodding, starting to jot down notes, then stopping, all the while his long forehead puckering and twitching, his jaw going slack, then his mouth dropping open, until finally he said, "Thanks, Henrik. We'll be in touch," and hung up. He stared at Elvis, chewing on his lower lip.

"What'd he say?" Elvis said.

"None of it . . . none of it appears to be stolen goods," Murphy began slowly. "But most of it is insured. Heavily insured."

"By who? Does he know?" Elvis asked.

Murphy did some more lip-chewing.

"He needs to do some double-checking," he said quietly.

"What the *heck* did he say, Murphy?" Elvis said, raising his voice.

Just then Regis came sailing back in the door, freshly shaven, his hair slicked back, and an expression of happy resolve on his patrician face. The man seemed to spin around a hundred and eighty degrees on a regular basis. Murphy looked from Regis to Elvis to the tips of his well-worn shoes.

"Nothing," Murphy mumbled to Elvis. "He didn't say anything important."

"I think we deserve dinner, boss," Regis declared cheerfully.

It was dark, Littlejon was probably safe for the night at least, Grieves would be near impossible to track down at this hour, and Elvis hadn't eaten a thing since his complimentary donut and coffee at the Stardust Cabins in Yosemite some sixteen hours ago.

"My treat," Elvis said.

In the spirit of his renewed resolve, Regis waved off the large pitcher of sangria that the waiter automatically brought to their table at La Cucina. Instead, he told the waiter to just bring out whatever dishes were ready to serve and to keep them coming until they screamed for him to stop.

"I wonder what Squirm's doing tonight," Elvis said, as he dipped his first chunk of bread into the guacamole.

"Sitting in a tree and howling at the moon," Regis said wistfully.

Murphy cocked his head and smiled. He seemed to have emerged from the nervous funk brought on by his phone conversation with the jeweler.

"You sounded like Fats Waller just then, Elvis," he said. "Fat's always ends his last set by saying, 'I wonder what the poor people is doin' tonight. And I wish I was doing it too.'"

"Good man, Fats," Elvis said.

"Good eater too," Regis said as a double portion of *albóndigas en chipotle* was deposited in the center of their table.

In the corner of Elvis's eye, Squirm's face suddenly flashed on the screen of the television set over the bar. Elvis immediately stood, jarring the table and knocking one of the *albóndigas* out of the serving dish, then limped over to the bar to listen, but the story was finishing up by the time he got there. Several of the drinkers were laughing.

"What's new about Littlejon?" Elvis asked them.

"He just have his dinner, Señor Presley," one of the drinkers said, grinning and raising his beer in a toast. "To Squirm-ay! *El bandito diminuto!*"

"Squirm-ay!" his companions echoed.

"One person see him eating steak at a restaurant up in Oildale," the first man said. "Another person see him eating tacos down in Grapevine. Either way, *el bandito diminuto*, he eating good."

"Gracias," Elvis said, and he returned to the table feeling more optimistic than he had all day. Not only did Squirm still have the authorities baffled, but he seemed to be evolving into a folk hero in the process. God love *el bandito diminuto*!

Elvis and his friends ate nonstop for over two hours.

They saw the envelope leaning against the wall of Regis's door as they came to the top of the stairs at ten thirty. It was a large manila job with a metal clip holding down the flap, ELVIS in newspaper letters was taped to the front. Somebody had clipped out his name from the morning's headlines.

Regis handed the envelope to Elvis, unlocked his door, and flipped on the lights. Elvis limped over to Regis's desk and heaved himself into the chair. He turned the envelope over in his hands uneasily. The way they'd stuck his cut-out name on it made it look like a ransom note in the movies.

It turned out to be worse than a ransom note. Much worse.

The first piece of paper Elvis withdrew was also written in letters clipped from a newspaper:

STOP SNOOP NOW OR THIS GOES PUBLIC

The second piece of paper was thicker. A contact sheet of 35mm black-and-white photographs. Elvis had to bring it up to his nose to make out the images: photographs of Ann-Margret and himself. *Naked.*

Elvis began to tremble. His gut churned. He felt dizzy. He squeezed his eyes shut and opened them again, but when he looked at the contact sheet the images remained the same: Ann-Margret and him making love.

Most of the little squares were fuzzy, out of focus. And many were at bizarre angles—a stretch of thigh jutting from one edge of the frame to the other; the bottom of a single foot; a giant elbow filling the entire frame. But scattered among these were three or four photographs that unmistakably revealed the faces and bodies of both Elvis and Miss Ann.

In the corner of one of the shots, Elvis glimpsed a piece of sheet music on the edge of a table, but it was too small to make out the song. In another, he saw the top of a race-car helmet, the one he wore to play Lucky Jackson in *Viva Las Vegas*. In another, the skimpy top of a swimsuit hanging from a plastic doorknob. Elvis recognized the knob; it was on the door to his location trailer in Vegas. The photographs must have been taken through a crack in the curtains of that trailer window.

The cramp in Elvis's gut turned vicious. He could kill whoever took these pictures. Kill whoever was blackmailing him with them.

Kill him with his bare hands. Wring his neck and watch his eyes pop out without feeling a shred of guilt.

"What is it, Elvis?" Murphy asked tentatively from the other side of the room.

Automatically, Elvis pressed the photo sheet against his chest.

"Nothing," he mumbled.

Nobody could see those pictures. *Never!* Not just Priscilla—*Nobody!* At that moment, Elvis would murder anyone who even *looked* at them. Murphy. Regis. Anybody. Kill them right there on the spot. Tear their eyes out after viewing that filth.

"You don't look too good," Regis said, sitting down behind his desk opposite Elvis.

"Shut your mouth!" Elvis barked.

Elvis stuffed the contact sheet back into the envelope, the blackmail note after it. It wasn't just what this would do to him and Priscilla. Not just the public disgrace either, even though that would surely send his career into a tailspin. It went way beyond that. It went straight to his mother's grave. Because it was *shame*. Ungodly *shame*. The *shame* of sullying all that was good and decent about being Gladys Presley's sole surviving son. The *shame* of being pornography. Yes, that is exactly what this made him—pornographic filth. Just like some of those church people had been saying about him all along, that all his hip wiggling had nothing to do with music and everything to do with sex. Wanton sex. Public sex. *Filthy* sex.

Without thinking, Elvis reached into his jacket pocket and pulled out the vial of painkillers. He screwed off the top and shook out a pill. Then another.

"Don't!" Regis blurted.

"Leave me alone."

"It'll ruin your life, my friend," Regis said beseechingly. He lunged across the desk, reaching for Elvis's hand. But he was too late. Elvis popped the two pills into his mouth and chewed them down.

"Quitter!"

But already Elvis could barely hear him.

21

THE ANGEL OF DEATH

IT WAS unlike any dream he'd ever had. Crystal clear. No shadows. No one thing turning into another thing without rhyme or reason. Everything was exactly what it was and nothing else. Elvis was Elvis. And Jesse Garon was Jesse Garon.

Jesse sat across from Elvis at the Formica-topped table, his hands in manacles.

"Greedy bastard!" Jesse snarled, rattling his chains. "One life to a customer. You wanted to have it all. Two of everything. Two homes. Two careers. Two women. Two feelings about every little thing. Fame *and* solitude. Sex *and* saintliness. Madonnas *and* whores."

"I'm working it out, Jesse. It ain't easy living for the two of us."

"My turn now. You had your chance and you blew it."

"*I* blew it?" Elvis hissed. "You couldn't even get yourself born!"

"Like I had a chance. You tried to kill me from the git go. Choke the life out of me before I took my first breath."

"Not possible," Elvis said. "Dr. Garcia says that—"

"*Dr. Garcia?*" Jesse snapped back. "Where the hell was he when you strung that umbilical cord around my neck? Counting specks in the jungle?"

"I wouldn't kill you, Jesse," Elvis pleaded. "I swear on Momma's grave."

"You're killing me now, Elvis," Jesse Garon said softly. "Killing me with shame."

"I'm sorry, Jesse. You don't know how sorry. But sometimes you got to choose between one shame and the other."

"My turn, Elvis," Jesse repeated in a whisper. "You blew it."

Elvis's eyes snapped open. His face and chest were sopped with sweat. His head ached. A cramp in his neck.

Blue neon light flashed on and off in Regis's window from Rodriguez's sign in the next window over. In the far corner, Regis was sprawled on his back on a fold-out army cot, wheezing and snoring alternately. No sign of Murphy. Elvis looked at his watch—6:10.

The photographs! Where were the photographs?

Elvis lurched out of his chair in a panic. The manila envelope skittered off his lap onto the floor. He picked it up, opened it, felt inside without looking. Two sheets, one thick, one thin. Still there.

Elvis crept out of the office without waking Regis, leaving his crutches leaning against the wall. He limped down the stairs to the street and made his way to La Cucina, which was either already open or still open from the previous night. He downed two quick *cafés con leche* at the bar, then headed for his car.

It was not quite seven o'clock when Elvis pulled up to the MGM gates. The guard studied him for a good thirty seconds before waving him through. Looking in his rearview mirror, Elvis could see why: the patchwork of stubble, the bloodshot eyes, the matted hair. He looked more like a stuntman than a movie star.

He parked at the north end of the lot, stuffing the manila envelope under his seat before locking the doors. Not another car within a hundred yards. He picked up the walkway behind Sound Studio G and turned left toward the outer campus. His left ankle sent a jolt of pain straight up to his hip every time he put his weight on it. Not a good time to take a pill, even though Regis made way too much of a fuss over the darned things. They were a doctor's prescription, for godssake.

Sighting the stunt shack, Elvis was reminded again of a Tennessee moonshine hut. One time Scotty had made a stop at one he knew near Brownsville after they'd played a high school jamboree over there. Elvis hadn't taken a drink, of course, but he remembered liking the smell of the place, kind of like wilted roses on a compost heap.

No action anywhere near the shack. Same stuff as before leaning against the wall—muskets, lances, Samurai swords. Somebody had taken the mini trampoline in for the night. Elvis approached the shack slowly, looking from side to side. He didn't see a soul.

The door was unlocked. Elvis slipped in quickly and closed the door behind him. Pitch black in here save for one thin line of morning sunlight cutting through a crack in the wall. Elvis stumbled over something—snorkeling gear, maybe—then felt his way along the wall until he touched the curtain to the bunk room. He stood perfectly still, listening. Nothing. Nobody home.

Inside the bunk room, Elvis edged to the closest cot and let himself down on it. His shirt was sticky from sweat, his face hot and prickly. His three days in the same clothes odor was wicked, but got lost in the smell of the dirty laundry scattered on the bunk-room floor. Elvis leaned back against the wall and waited.

This is where it all began. Where Holly set up her little operation, her hedge against the precariousness of show business. And this is where she had been strangled to death with a strip of rubber tubing. Done in by a guilt-crazed customer, if Mike Murphy's theory was right—a guilt-crazed customer with powerful connections. That's what it all came down to, didn't it? Sex and power. Madonnas and whores.

A tremor twisted down Elvis's spine. They wouldn't have any trouble getting a newspaper to run the photographs of him and Ann-Margret. Maybe not the *L.A. Times* or the *Hollywood Reporter*, but the *National Enquirer* would grab them in a minute. *Silver Screen* too. Sure, they'd discreetly blot out their privates—after all, they're responsible periodicals, not pornographic publications. But then what? The church folk would be all over the story, wagging their fingers and smugly saying, "I told you so. Elvis is the devil himself, incarnate." Then the studios would fall in line, dissolving their contracts with him in the name of human decency. *Hollywood* decency.

RCA might hang in for a while. The Colonel would convince them that the whole business would increase record sales, and he'd probably be right at that. Kids would be listening to "Big Hunk o' Love" with visions of Elvis and Ann-Margret dancing in their heads. The very thought made him want to break his record contract himself.

And then? What do you do with the rest of your life after you've been Elvis Presley? Go back to driving a truck in West Tennessee, singing to yourself in the cabin? Would that be so bad? Just a few days back he'd been musing wistfully about that writer who faked his death and changed his name so he could get his real life back.

He heard whistling outside. "If You Knew Suzie." Closer, louder, now footsteps too. Elvis stood, crept toward the curtain. The whistler broke into song, "Oh, Oh, Oh what a gal!" *Grieves.*

Elvis sucked in his breath, pressed himself against the wall to the right of the curtain. The shack door opened, a shaft of bright sunlight appeared on the curtain, then squeezed down to a stripe, and then it was dark again.

"There's none so classy, as this fair lassy. Oh, Oh—"

Click. On the other side of the curtain the overhead lights snapped on. Whistling again. Cheery, oh so cheery. "Oh, what a gal."

Elvis's eyes darted around the now dimly illuminated bunk room. In the corner, out of reach, a horsewhip. He lowered himself onto his knees, crawled soundlessly over a carpet of discarded T-shirts to the corner, grasped the whip, then crawled back to the curtain. At the bottom edge, there was a tiny break between curtain and wall. Still on his knees, Elvis craned down his head, his chin touching the floor, and positioned a single eye at the break. He could only see Grieves from the waist down.

I am a camera, Elvis thought, *spying through a crack in the curtain.*

Grieves was pulling down his pants, singing aloud again. "Holy Moses, what a chassis!"

I am a film maker, Elvis thought, *making a pornographic movie.*

Grieves was now pulling on some kind of skin-tight leggings. Wisps of feathers floating down to his ankles. It was that rubber body suit Elvis had seen when Will Cathcart brought him in here, the one with feathers fastened to the front and back like some kind of giant seabird. The monster movie.

Grieves abruptly disappeared from view. Elvis raised himself onto his feet, bracing himself with the horsewhip. He placed a finger at the edge of the curtain, creating a tiny new opening at eye level. Grieves was paddling in the bird suit to where the roof shot up a dozen feet to accommodate the nylon cable that supported the leather chest-and-shoulder harness. Nelly, the stuntman's mistress.

Grieves was singing to himself again, "We went riding/She didn't balk/ Back from Yonkers/ I'm the one who had to walk." He backed into the harness as if a valet was holding his coat for him, then quickly attached the buckles and skillfully tied the corset-like laces in back by reaching both hands behind him. He was, after all, the master stuntman.

Elvis now saw that Grieves had knotted the pull end of the cable to his ankle. Grieves untied it, wrapped it around his left hand, then began drawing against the pulley with both hands, lifting himself off of the ground. Hand over hand, he elevated himself more than halfway to the ceiling, a good eight feet up. Then, slinging his legs forward like a child on a playground swing, he swung forward, folded his legs and swung back, then forward again to the wall where he grabbed a beam. With a single graceful toss, he looped the end of the cable around a hook on the wall, secured it with a slipknot, released both cable and beam, and swung back. Grieves was flying solo now. He spread his feathered arms, swooping in a circle like an enormous falcon scouting for prey, ready to pounce with its lethal talons.

Elvis slipped furtively through the curtain, made his way into the harness room without being seen or heard. He was now standing directly under Grieves.

"Fine day for flying, isn't it, Mickey?" Elvis called up to him.

Grieves spun around, gaped down, then immediately started pumping his legs, swinging himself toward the hook where the cable was tied. He reached out with his right hand, grasping for the slipknot. But just as he touched the cable, Elvis raised the horsewhip and snapped it, the tip lashing against the back of Grieves's outstretched hand, instantly drawing blood. Grieves reflexively pulled back his hand, spun in a half turn, then smacked against the wall, the hook tearing through his rubber suit at the shoulder and cutting into his skin. A handful of feathers wafted down like autumn leaves.

"I know you killed Will," Elvis called up to him. "Know all about the bull and the pork insulin. Got proof. Got witnesses."

Grieves said nothing. He suddenly started to swing back toward the hook, but Elvis shot out the whip again, lashed it around one of

Grieves's ankles and held tight. It arrested Grieves in mid-swing, far short of the hook.

"The question is, did you kill Holly too?" Elvis went on. "Or are you just doing someone's bidding? Covering somebody else's mess?"

"Who the hell do you think you are, Pelvis?" Grieves shouted back. "You're just a one-note warbler that got lucky. But it can all come tumbling down in a minute. Just like that, and you're a nobody again."

"That's true," Elvis said evenly. "Never been more aware of that in my life. But the thing is, Mickey, I'd rather be a nobody than turn my eyes away from evil. I know that for sure now."

Grieves cackled.

"Oh, they're going to get you good, Pelvis," he snarled. "You're going to be worse than a nobody. Worse than a has-been. You're going to be scum."

"You talking about the pictures, right?" Elvis said. "The photographs?"

"Yeh, the pictures. You and your movie star playing pattycake in the trailer." Grieves cackled again. "Trailer trash!"

Elvis snapped the whip, catching Grieves just below the harness on his rump. It made him spin like a Christmas-tree ornament on a ribbon. Grieves grimaced with pain.

"Who are *they*, Mickey?" Elvis said. "Who's trying to stop me?"

"It doesn't matter *who*,'" Grieves called back. "It's *what they can do*. And that's just about anything they feel like doing."

"I know what Holly was doing out here," Elvis said. "And I know it's one of her johns who's behind all this. Give me his name, Grieves. Give me the name or I'm going to call the police right now and have them come get you for Will's murder."

"They won't believe you, Pelvis," Grieves said. "Hell, they never believe a drug addict."

Elvis swallowed hard. "They'll believe the vet who did the autopsy on the bull," he said. "And they'll believe Binxter Bartley who saw you give it that shot." That wasn't exactly the truth, but for emphasis Elvis snapped the whip under Grieves's chin.

For a long moment, Grieves said nothing. Then, "Okay. Let me down and I'll tell you. I'll tell you who killed Holly. But then you got to let me run. Get a running start before you call the police."

"Deal," Elvis said.

Above him, Grieves started to pump his legs, swinging toward the hook and slipknot. He folded his feathered arms across his chest like a bashful angel. A sudden silver flash appeared in his hand.

A shriek: *"You killed my Willy!"*

Elvis spun around. Jilly-Jo Cathcart had soundlessly crept into the stunt shack. She stood just behind Elvis, a long-handled stunt apparatus held high in her hands. Squeeze trigger at one end, a spring, a length of rubber tubing, huge scissor-like blades at the other.

One well-placed snip is all it took.

Grieves was in mid-swing when she snapped the cable. A sudden look of horror, then a dark smile as he spread his wings, swooping toward Elvis with his right hand raised. The silver flash was a knife in his hand.

Elvis jumped to his right. Grieves knocked against Elvis's left shoulder, flipped, and hit the floor on his belly. That was it. Grieves didn't move. A stream of purple blood trickled out from under his chest. Elvis and Jilly-Jo stared down at him. Then Elvis stooped down and pulled Grieves up by the shoulders. The handle of the knife was still in Grieves's right hand; the blade was deep in his chest. He was dead.

Jilly-Jo was shaking, sobbing uncontrollably. Elvis put his arm across her shoulders.

"We best get out of here," he whispered.

They started for the shack door. Abruptly, Elvis halted, turned, and again leaned over Grieves's sprawling corpse. He quickly withdrew the tweezers from his jacket pocket, yanked a strand of bloodied hair from the back of Grieves's head, and then stuck both tweezers and hair into his pocket.

Five minutes later, Elvis drove out through the MGM gate with Jilly-Jo crouched behind the driver's seat and hidden under Elvis's jacket. Elvis knew full well that he was abetting the escape of a murderer, but sometimes you got to choose between one shame and the other. Funny thing was, being connected to the death of Mickey Grieves didn't feel like a shame at all.

22
THE SILENCE BETWEEN VERSES

SENOR Rodriguez was adjusting the rabbit-ears aerial of an eight-inch television on Regis's desk when Elvis walked in the door. Electrified by a series of extension cords that led back to the travel agency, the set appeared to be pulling in three stations simultaneously, one black-and-white image of a newscaster layered over the other, which seemed appropriate for its tripartite audience. Regis, Delores Suarez, and Hector Garcia sat about as far away from each other as the tiny office permitted, and there was enough static electricity being generated between them to interfere with reception in the entire building.

"So where have *you* been, Elvis?" Regis said, staring at the fluttering screen.

"Condolence call," Elvis replied. "Out in Maywood to see Jilly-Jo Cathcart."

The only part that was true about that, of course, was that he had driven Jilly-Jo home to Maywood from MGM. On the way, she had explained that Binxter Bartley had phoned her right after he had spoken with Elvis. She had come to the stunt shack that morning with the intention of confronting Grieves, not killing him. But when she had seen Grieves draw that knife in mid-air, she had reacted spontaneously. She had simply done what she had to do, she said; she had never intended to kill Grieves. Elvis and Jilly-Jo decided that for now they would not tell anyone what had transpired in the stunt shack.

But what was going on *here*? Hector Garcia had not even glanced at Elvis since he entered the room.

"Wonderful to see you, Hector," Elvis said, walking toward him with his hand extended. "Glad you could get up here so quick."

"I came in good faith," the doctor said quietly, his eyes cast down, his own hands remaining rigidly at his side.

"I know that, Dr. Garcia, and I truly appreciate it," Elvis said. He gazed at the doctor, bewildered. "I've made all the arrangements for a lab and a place for you to stay."

Delores turned her coal-black eyes from the television screen and glared at Elvis accusingly.

"We know about your drug problem, Elvis," she said.

"My *what*?"

"Your codeine addiction," Delores said.

"I had to tell them after the police came here looking for you," Regis jumped in. "Prime suspect in the murder of Mickey Grieves. It's the only defense we've got. Drug-induced rage, insanity defense. It's either that or you start running now. The police are looking for you everywhere."

"But I didn't kill Grieves!" Elvis bellowed.

"They have a witness," Delores blurted. "The guard at the gates. He saw you go in there just before Grieves arrived."

"I . . . I was there when it happened," Elvis stammered. "But it was . . . it was an accident."

"An *accident*," Regis echoed.

Elvis heard the wail of a siren in the distance. His head was spinning. He suddenly dropped to his knees in front of Hector Garcia and looked up at him beseechingly.

"I swear on the grave of my mother that I did not kill that man," Elvis said. "You can believe me or not believe me, but please, Doctor, take the samples. Do the lab work. Help me find the truth."

For an interminable moment, Dr. Hector Garcia gazed deeply into Elvis's eyes. "You must make me a promise," he said, finally.

"Anything."

"No more drugs," the doctor said. "No more codeine, even if you are in pain."

"But I am not a drug ad—" Elvis stopped himself, then, "Yes, Doctor. I promise."

Garcia stood. "I will get to work immediately," he said. "But I believe you must go now."

Elvis quickly jotted down Dr. Belizzi's number at the UCLA laboratory. He suddenly remembered the tweezers and hair in his pocket and handed it to Garcia, explaining that it was from Grieves. He started for the door, but Delores stopped him.

"I will need a sample from you also," she said, a laboratory vial in her hand.

"What in heck for?"

"Elimination," Delores Suarez said. "In case you have contaminated any of the samples by handling them. I will take cells from Regis and from your Mr. Murphy also." She reached up and plucked a hair from Elvis's head.

"Elvis?" Regis was now standing beside Elvis too, but he was unable to look at him directly. His bloodshot eyes kept darting around the office, his lips were quivering. He looked like he needed a drink very badly.

"What is it, Regis?" Elvis said.

"I . . . I am sorry if I . . . if I spoke out of turn about . . . about your drug problem," Regis stammered. "But I worry about you."

"And I worry about you, Regis," Elvis said.

"I am not going to have another drink myself, Elvis," Regis said. "I promise you that."

Delores suddenly took Regis's hand and squeezed it.

"You two take care of each other," Elvis said, and he left.

Mike Murphy's timing was perfect again. He was just pulling his shiny black Corvair coupe up to the curb when Elvis emerged from Regis's building.

"Keep the motor running, Murph," Elvis said, pulling open the passenger door and easing himself in. "I need to stay in motion."

"So I hear," Murphy said, slipping his car back into first gear. "Police have an all-points going for you. But they've made the press keep a lid on it for now. There's enough in the news about you as it is."

"I didn't kill Grieves," Elvis said.

"Glad to hear that," Murphy said, nosing the car into the traffic. "It would make for kind of an abrupt ending to your biography."

"So what *are* they saying in the news about me?"

"You haven't heard?"

Elvis put his hand to his forehead. My God, had they published those photographs in the papers already? "Haven't heard a thing," he said.

"Warden Reardon has been relieved of his duties out at CCI," Murphy said. "But that's the least of his problems. They're indicting him for unlawfully releasing Squirm Littlejon. They say he aided and abetted his escape."

"We're way ahead of them on that one," Elvis said, feeling only half relieved. "But what's that got to do with me?"

Murphy chuckled. "One of the guards out at the prison has come forward and declared that Reardon did it expressly for you. Because you are a personal friend of his and of Squirm's. But mostly because Reardon wants you to make some movie of his."

"The Singing Warden," Elvis said.

"Jesus!" Murphy said. "You mean they're right?"

"They're right about Reardon's movie," Elvis said. "Wrong about him letting Squirm loose for me. I knew they'd hang Reardon out to dry if thing's didn't go according to their plan, but I never figured on this—trying to hang him and me at the same time."

Murphy turned onto Santa Monica Boulevard. "Where are we going, by the way?" he said.

"Any place they won't come looking for me," Elvis said, then, "I take it Squirm is still out there or they wouldn't be turning on Reardon."

"Oh, Squirm's out there, all right," Murphy said, grinning. "So far he's been spotted in Pacific Palisades, El Paso, Tijuana, and Montreal. And he was seen by an entire family wriggling out of a drainpipe in downtown Spokane. Family said they shared a hero sandwich with him and wished him well on his journey."

"El bandito diminuto!" Elvis cheered.

"I saved the best for last," Murphy went on. "Squirm was sighted in a White Tower on the south side of Chicago where he was sharing a bag of burgers with *you*."

Elvis laughed. "Hey, why not? They had me in a London hotel with Ann-Margret just a couple of days ago. Man, I could be dead and buried and they'd still be spotting me all over the map."

A sudden flash of red light shot in through the Corvair's slanted back window.

"Damn! The cops!" Murphy cried. "I got to pull over. Hide!"

"Hide?" The coupe was tinier than the cabin of an eight-wheeler, the narrow rear seat jutting within inches of the front bucket seats.

"Pull up the carpet!" Murphy said, pointing at the floor pan under Elvis's feet.

Elvis did as he was told. Under the carpet was a hinged panel. He pulled it open as Murphy coasted onto the shoulder, the police car right behind him. The opening led directly under the car's hood.

"I'll burn to a crisp in there!" Elvis said.

"Engine's in rear," Murphy said. "Go! *Now!*"

Elvis slid down in his seat, wiggling through feet first. When he got down to his hips, he stuck, too wide for the opening. Murphy kept on coasting. The cops blared their horn. *What would Squirm do?*

Elvis twisted clockwise, then twisted back, doing a little slithery thing with his hips like he did when he performed "Teddy Bear." He gyrated into the Corvair's front luggage compartment and pulled the panel shut just as Murphy came to a full stop. Above his head, he heard Murphy kick the carpet back down over the floor pan.

"Was I speeding, Officer?" Murphy intoned, sounding like the male equivalent of a Santa Monica housewife on her way to the beauty salon.

"I thought it was you, Murphy," Elvis heard the policeman reply. "Nobody else would be seen dead in one of these pickle wagons."

"It's the car of the future, Officer."

"I hear you've been hanging out with Elvis lately," the policeman said.

"That's right," Murphy replied brightly. "I'm his official biographer."

"So where is he, Mr. Biographer?"

"Last I heard he was in Chicago—South Chicago, actually. Supping with Squirm Littlejon."

"Don't get wise with me, Murphy."

"Honest, I heard it on the radio."

"And you believe that, right?" the policeman whined sarcastically.

"Well, it was on the *news*."

"Listen, Murphy, if you know where he is and don't tell, we can put you away for a long time."

"I'm a law-abiding citizen, Officer," Murphy said. "If I were you, I'd put in a call to Chicago's finest real quick."

A moment later, they were rolling again, Murphy cackling, "Come out, come out, wherever you are, Elvis!"

Crouched fetal-like on his side under the Corvair's hood, Elvis smiled. There was something surprisingly tranquil about lying here in the semi-darkness, bouncing along in this cramped enclosure. Outside, he was Missing Elvis, Wanted-for-Murder Elvis, Phantom Elvis Eating Two-Bite Burgers with Squirm, Drug-Crazed Elvis, Pornographic Elvis Making Love to a Swedish Starlet. But in the luggage compartment of Mike Murphy's coupe, he was just himself, Elvis from Tupelo, Gladys Presley's little boy with the soulful voice.

"I'd rather stay in here, Murph," he called back.

"Fine with me. Next stop, the *L.A. Times*. Got a room there nobody comes looking in. The Caboose."

The room was in a sub basement under the presses, and Murphy had been using it for years as his personal getaway from the sea of desks and wiseguys in the newsroom. It was outfitted with a desk and chair, a phone, a radio, and a ratty sofa. No windows, no pictures on the walls. Pictures would have tumbled off their hooks anyway—the incessant overhead rumble of the presses made the room vibrate like a railway car. Elvis stretched out on the sofa.

"By the way, it turned out I was right about that Aronson woman," Murphy said, sitting down at his desk and pulling a yellowed newspaper out of the middle drawer. "I *had* seen her before. When I was a cub on courthouse duty back in fifty-eight."

Elvis sat up. "What was she doing in court?"

"Smiling like the Cheshire cat," Murphy answered. "She'd been arrested for solicitation."

"You're kidding me."

"Not for herself, of course," Murphy went on, unfolding the newspaper. "Miss Aronson has always been in management."

"She was soliciting for someone else?"

"For a whole stable of call girls," Murphy said. "Twenty or thirty of them. Mostly moonlighting chorus girls and bit players."

"Like Miss Holly," Elvis said.

"Yes, like Holly," Murphy said.

"You said she was smiling."

"That's right, the smile of an untouchable. Aronson knew there was no way in hell she would have to pay for her sins."

"Why's that?"

"Her black book," Murphy said. "She took it out of her I. Magnum pocketbook and flashed it at the judge like it was the devil's own amulet. Her client list."

"Who was on it, Murph?"

Murphy laughed. "That's what everybody wanted to know. A list of names like that can skyrocket a cub reporter's career in a single edition of the morning paper. The judge took one look at it, turned several shades of purple, and handed it back to Miss Aronson like it was molten lead burning his fingers. Must have been some major bigwigs on that list." Murphy snapped his fingers. "Case dismissed, just like that."

"On what grounds?"

"Coffee grounds," Murphy said, laughing again. "Insufficient fiddle-di-di. The usual mumbo jumbo they come up with when they want to smother a hot potato. She was out of there in a flash. But not before the intrepid reporter, Michael Xavier Murphy, could snap her picture." He held the newspaper aloft, pointing to a tiny photograph in the corner of a page next to an advertisement for a funeral home. "It's what's known in the trade as a buried story."

Elvis leaned forward on the sofa. The dismissed case of Miss Maryjane Aronson occupied a mere one-and-a-half column inches on page thirty-six of the newspaper, wedged—without so much as a subhead—between a report about one Ralph Lulek's bail bond and one Suzy "Tootsie" Peppard's thirty-day-suspended sentence for "loitering with intent," although it didn't specify what her intent might have been. The photograph was a tiny gray smudge without a caption; the way it was placed, one would surmise that it was of Tootsie herself, caught in the act of loitering.

"How the heck did Miss Aronson get from there to the movie business?" Elvis asked.

"Probably through the front door," Murphy answered. "I imagine that black book has opened a lot of doors for her. Soft-core blackmail."

"I bet there's a connection between her and Miss Holly," Elvis said.

"I'm sure there is," Murphy said. "Maybe Holly wasn't the independent contractor we assumed she was. But there's more, Elvis." Murphy began rummaging around in the middle desk drawer and pulled out another section of newspaper. This one looked whiter, more recent. "I did a search in the morgue for anything else we may have run about Maryjane Aronson. And lo and behold, this turned up in the business section last May."

Murphy folded the paper into quarters and held it up close to his eyes.

"Small print, straight from the rolls of the state office of revenue and taxation. The week's new corporations." Murphy traced a finger down a column, then began to read, "'Incorporated April 20, 1963, Timeless Films, a motion-picture studio. CEO, Miss Maryjane Aronson. Initial capitalization, six million dollars.' It says they'll be open for business in January 1964. That's just a few months from now."

"Holy Moses!" Elvis said. "She told me she was going to be making pictures on her own. Pictures Miss Pollard couldn't dream of making."

"Yup, she's starting up her own movie studio, and I'll tell you, six million bucks is a lot of capital for a nobody in this town," Murphy said. "Not even a Hollywood madame earns that kind of moolah. It seems little Miss Maryjane has investors—that's in the small print too, although it doesn't give any names, of course. But I'd bet the farm that you could find every one of those investors in her little black book. Miss Aronson gives new meaning to the idea that whore mongers run Hollywood."

Elvis started limping up and down the Caboose.

"Man, it's all connected, isn't it?" he murmured. "Aronson, Holly, Squirm. It's like Regis says, 'It's a puzzle wrapped in an enigma.'"

Murphy smiled. "You can say that again, Elvis. But I don't know where we go from here."

Elvis kept pacing.

"I suppose we could get to work on your biography," Murphy ventured brightly. "I mean, it doesn't look like you're going anywhere at the moment."

Elvis came to a sudden halt.

"Let's give her a call," he said.

"Who?"

"Miss Aronson. Call her up and say I want to talk business."

"What kind of business, Elvis?"

"The only kind she knows, Murph. Show business." Elvis sat down on the corner of the desk, lifted the phone, dialed MGM, then proffered the receiver to Murphy. "Tell the operator you want to talk to Aronson in Development."

Murphy took the phone. The operator apparently asked who was calling and Murphy replied, "Sol, from the William Morris Agency. She'll know who it is." Grinning, he handed the phone back to Elvis.

"Development. Miss Aronson speaking."

"Afternoon, Miss Aronson. It's Elvis."

Not a sound in response. Hank Snow once told Elvis that the silences between verses were the loudest part of a song. This one screamed.

"I hear you're opening up your own picture studio, and I was thinking about what you said at Will Cathcart's funeral," Elvis went on blithely. "You know, about me being like James Dean in *Rebel Without a Cause* and all. Did you really mean that, ma'am?"

The blaring silence continued. Elvis could hear every little thought crackling through Miss Aronson's fine-wired brain. She knew Grieves was dead and she knew that Elvis was suspected of doing it. They might be able to keep a story like that out of the press for now, but there is no way they could keep it from circulating at MGM. She probably also guessed that Elvis was in hiding somewhere. On top of that, she undoubtedly realized that Elvis was starting to put things together: Mickey Grieves and Will Cathcart's death; maybe even her career as solicitor to the rich and famous in the call-girl business.

But rising above the din of every one of those thoughts was the fact that Elvis Presley, the most bankable star in the universe, was phoning *her*—Maryjane Aronson, the head of a fledgling movie studio. Of all the timeless truths that Elvis had learned in Hollywood, the one he was banking on now was that a deal—a big-time movie deal—was worth absolutely any risk. Such was the power and the weakness of the Hollywood mind-set.

"Yes, I meant that, Elvis," Aronson said finally. "You have a special quality that none of your films has ever touched. A kind of vulnerability mixed with grit. James Dean meets Gary Cooper. And we aren't even talking about your singing."

"You figure I could carry a film without singing a single song?"

"I most certainly do, Elvis." Aronson was at full tilt now, all fast-talking charm and flattery. And *promises*. Promise anything, close the deal, worry later. If she had a single qualm about murder or blackmail or the possibility of spending enough time in prison for her hair to return to its natural color and *then* turn white, the prospect of closing a deal with Elvis Presley trumped it without a whisper of internal protest. What the heck, her black book had kept her out of jail before. And she knew from experience that genuinely powerful men were immune from prosecution, even for murder. That would include Elvis himself—nothing as trivial as suspicion of a lowly stuntman's murder could prevent the King from appearing in Timeless Films' first major motion picture.

"Well, I surely would like to make a real moving picture for a change," Elvis said in the earnest tones of a veteran actor. "Something that would give the folks something meaningful to talk about on their way out of the theater."

"I know you would," Aronson said. "And that is exactly what I want to do too. We are in absolute agreement about that."

"Well, I guess we should get together then and talk turkey," Elvis said.

"Yes, turkey," Aronson said.

"I could meet you this evening," Elvis said.

"Yes, that would be nice," Aronson said. She hesitated a moment, then, "I don't think over here at MGM would be appropriate. We both want privacy, don't we?"

"Yes, ma am."

"How about my new offices?" Aronson said. "They're a little primitive at the moment. Just bare-bones furnishings. But I'm sure we can manage."

"Sounds perfect," Elvis said.

Aronson gave him an address in Studio City.

"I'll see you at eight, then. Alone," she said. "And Elvis?"

"Yes?"

"Should I order in?"

"No, ma'am," Elvis said. "I kinda lost my appetite lately."

23
A TWO-BLACKMAIL DEAL

ELVIS brought a pillow with him this time. Back under the hood of the Corvair, he curled up like a caterpillar in a cocoon in the fresh clothes Murphy had found for him. Elvis rested his head on the pillow and that feeling of peace descended on him again. The womb must have felt like this—close and secure, noisy movement outside, protective stillness inside. There was just enough room for another man his size to curl up on the other side, his head where Elvis's feet were. Just enough room for Jesse Garon.

He had made two quick phone calls after speaking with Miss Aronson. First, he called Belizzi's laboratory at UCLA. Garcia and Suarez were already at work and things were going smoothly; they expected to have some results later that evening. Regis came on and again apologized to Elvis for talking out of turn about his codeine pills. Elvis told him to forget it; they had more important things to think about now. Then he asked how things were going between him and Delores, and Regis just sort of hummed in reply. It was a happy hum, the hum of a man who cannot believe his good fortune.

Next, Elvis had phoned Colonel Parker at his office at MGM.

"It's me, Colonel." Elvis automatically held the phone away from his ear: Parker's hyper-ventilated blare virtually drowned out the rumble of the presses above them.

"I'm dying, boy, you know that? You're killing me, Elvis! Do you know what they're saying about you now?"

"I know all about it," Elvis said calmly. "But don't you worry your pretty little head. Everything's going to work out fine. I just need a few more days to sort out a couple things."

"Damn it, Elvis, your pal Squirm is scot-free. Doing the hat dance in Mexico somewhere. That's what you wanted, so why can't you leave it be now? Then maybe—just *maybe*—we can salvage your career."

That was true, all right. It looked like Squirm really had wriggled his way to permanent freedom. Not only that, but Will Cathcart's death had been avenged, avenged with the ultimate retribution. If Elvis dropped the rest right here—STOP SNOOP NOW—those awful photos would be dropped too, and he really could get back to his life and his career. That is, once he cleared himself of Grieves's murder. Sometimes you've got to chose between one shame and another.

"Can't do it, Tom," Elvis said finally. "Got a couple more things to work out. But I want you to set up a press conference so I can tell everybody what's really been going on here. The whole truth. And then everything will be all hunky-dory again."

A long pause. "When?"

"How about Friday?" Elvis said. That gave him two more days to put this thing together, two more days to play tag with the police and his blackmailer. "Meantime, put it out there that I'm doing just fine, recuperating from a sprained ankle in a sanitorium somewhere in New Mexico. That should keep them busy looking for me somewhere else."

Parker grumbled. "You don't give me any choice, son. You're crazy, but I'll do it."

"And by the way, Colonel," Elvis said. "I didn't kill Grieves."

"I know that, boy. You'd never do a thing like that."

"And I didn't pull strings for Squirm's escape neither."

"I was wondering about that," the Colonel said.

"I would have," Elvis said. "Just didn't think of it."

Timeless Films, Incorporated, occupied the entire fifth floor of an art deco building on the south end of Ventura Boulevard. Elvis waited in the Corvair's luggage compartment for several minutes after the car stopped; then, when the coast was clear, Murphy popped the hood and escorted him through the entrance hidden under a billowing white parka that he'd brought along for the occasion. To any passerby, it may have looked like Murph was steering the casualty of a parachute accident toward the elevator, but it takes considerably more than that to cause the denizens of Ventura Boulevard to stop and stare.

Elvis took the elevator up alone. There was not a doubt in his mind that Maryjane Aronson was somehow involved in the murder of Holly McDougal. She probably had not choked Holly herself—that must have been done by Holly's final customer—but Aronson had surely participated in the cover-up and frame-up that put Squirm in jail for the murder. Aronson was one of the new Hollywood entrepreneurs, a woman with connections, an operator with a firm grasp of the art of the deal: *You scratch my back and I'll scratch yours.* Except the ante had been upped with this new generation: *You cover up my homicide and I'll bank your film studio.* For them, it was just a minor variation on the same principle.

Elvis had only the bare outlines of a plan for what he was going to say to Miss Aronson. Above all, he needed to find out who her investors were—the murderer would surely be on that list. But that would be like asking to see her little black book: most of the names were undoubtedly the same, and Aronson could never afford to reveal them. Those veiled names were the fulcrum on which her entire little empire was balanced, her amulet against harm, her passport to Hollywood's front offices. Maryjane Aronson had to believe that Elvis wanted something else from her.

Yup, that was the key, all right. On the countless occasions when the Colonel had numbingly lectured Elvis on the brilliance of his deal-making, he always declaimed the Tom Parker Golden Rule: Make the other party believe that you desperately want something that you actually didn't give a hoot about. That put you in the catbird seat; you could moan and groan about giving up something that was actually worthless to you, then turn around and get what you *really* wanted. Elvis usually tuned out these lectures—it was worth the Colonel's twenty-five percent just to spare himself the details of his conniving money games. But this little bit of Parker wisdom had stuck somehow. So the question was, What should the CEO of Timeless Films believe Elvis desperately wanted from her? It had to be something she thought Elvis Presley couldn't get from anyone else in Hollywood.

"Hi, there!"

Maryjane Aronson was standing directly in front of the elevator as the doors separated on the fifth floor. Her hair was a living advertisement for Clairol, her tailored gray skirt and navy blue blazer a testament to good taste and expendable income, and the expression on her aging-kitten face pure eagerness. She raised herself onto the toes of her calfskin pumps and planted noisy kisses on each of Elvis's cheeks. A Hollywood kiss, although it had gone by a different name in the Bible when they wrote up the Last Supper.

"Good evening, Ma'am."

Elvis looked beyond Aronson to the offices of Timeless Films. Indeed, there was no furniture yet on the maroon carpeted floors, just phones sitting on the floor and cardboard boxes lining the walls. Aronson led the way to her corner office, a spacious room with arching windows, a pair of folding chairs, a card table, more boxes, and, snugged in the far corner, the largest item, an antique brass safe that looked almost comical in here, like the safe in a "Tom and Jerry" cartoon that fell out the window and made a pancake out of a pedestrian below. Elvis peered at it. By God, that had to be it. Maryjane's little black book was in there. Her fortune of secret names all locked up.

"I can't tell you how excited I am about all of this," Aronson said, gesturing for Elvis to sit in one of the folding chairs.

"I am too, ma'am," Elvis replied, remaining standing.

"Please call me Maryjane." Aronson performed something that looked like a wink, but was hedged with an ironic smile. It was like those songs they wrote for him out here: half feeling, half parody of feeling.

"Sure thing," Elvis said. "I hope you don't mind if I get right down to business, Maryjane."

"Please do, Elvis." Aronson remained on her feet also.

"Well, like you know, I want to make meaningful films, important films, the kind Colonel Parker and Hal Wallis and just about everybody at MGM don't think I have in me."

"Exactly," Aronson replied, nodding emphatically.

"But if I had the right producer, somebody who really trusted me as an actor, you know, like James Dean, then I'd jump right in. Get rid of all those people who don't believe in me and make movies with somebody who really does."

"We are precisely on the same wavelength," Aronson bubbled. She could already see herself taking over the Colonel's entire franchise.

So far, it had been a piece of cake, basically because everything Elvis was saying he actually believed in. But now it was time to swoop in with the bamboozle, and it came to Elvis in an inspired Colonel Parker-like flash.

"So here's the film I want to make with you, Maryjane," Elvis said. "Dr. Freud: The Musical."

Aronson's tight little mouth momentarily dropped open, but she recovered immediately with an earnest smile. "A musical comedy, right?"

"No, ma'am," Elvis replied. "Serious. Kind of like an opera, you know?"

"And you—?"

"I'd play the good doctor, of course," Elvis continued, amazed at how effortlessly all of this was coming out of him and at how much he was enjoying it too. "I know Freud had some kind of accent. German, I think. But with practice, I could get my tongue around that, don't you think?"

Aronson braced both hands on the back of the folding chair in front of her.

"And I'd sing, you know?" Elvis went on rhapsodically. "The singing shrink. I even got a few songs worked out in my mind. One called, 'Taboo.' It's about sex, of course. And one called, 'Dress-up Games Rock.' You know, about the games people play to soup up their sex lives. And another one about loving your mamma. I call it, 'Madonnas and Whores.'"

Oh, yes, Regis's cram course in psychology was paying off in spades, spades and jokers. Maryjane Aronson, Hollywood madame and criminal co-conspirator, looked positively scandalized. In Hollywood, the rules about what was fit and proper to go on a movie screen were entirely different story from the rules about what was fit and proper to do in real life.

"I, uh, I like it, Elvis," Aronson stammered. "Very, uh, very unusual. Very original."

"Thank you, ma'am. So what do you say? Should we write up a contract right now? Make it happen before the Colonel tries to put the kibosh on it?"

Elvis watched Aronson's face twitch as she tried to figure out what to do next, as the bamboozle confused and befuddled her normally razor-sharp mind. *"Freud: The Musical"* was a totally ridiculous idea. Ridiculous and absolutely unbankable. But signing up Elvis Presley was a dream come true, a coup that could transform her piddling new studio into a major player overnight. Thoughts about everything else—Holly, Grieves, murder, cover-ups—were reduced to wisps of smoke.

"Are you, uh, married to this Freud idea?" Aronson asked tentatively.

"I ain't married to nobody," Elvis laughed, working up a naive Jodie Tatum look on his face. "Nobody and nothing."

"I mean, uh, are you saying we could discuss other movie ideas?" Aronson went on, trying to keep her excitement under control. "You know, just play around with them and see if we come up with something else? Maybe something even more compelling than the Freud opera?"

Elvis stroked his chin in a way that he hoped made him look deep in thought. He could practically hear the Colonel whispering in his ear: *Slow and easy, son. Make her squirm. Make her think that if she makes one false move, she blows the whole deal.*

"I sure do like that Freud idea, ma'am," Elvis drawled. "A real meaty part, you know?"

Aronson nodded, barely breathing.

"And I surely don't want to do any more films like *Kissin' Cousins*. Makes me look silly and feel ridiculous," Elvis went on. "That's why I like this new idea of mine. It's serious."

"I know, Elvis. I wouldn't even suggest something like *Kissin' Cousins*. You're far too talented for that. We'd have to come up with something totally serious and meaningful. Like one idea I've been playing with is a remake of *Rebel Without a Cause*, with you in the Dean part, of course."

Elvis did some more chin stroking and head scratching while Aronson virtually quivered in her pumps.

"That sure is an interesting idea, Maryjane," Elvis said at last. "Maybe we could do that first and the Freud movie next. Why don't we just put in the contract something like, 'for two scripts to be agreed upon later'? That should make us both happy, right?"

Tears of joy suddenly appeared in the corners of Maryjane Aronson's eyes. In just about any place else in the world, you would have looked at her beaming face and thought this woman had just been proposed to by the man of her dreams. But this was Studio City and the woman in question had just closed the movie deal of her dreams.

Aronson abruptly spun around, darted to one of the cardboard boxes against the wall, pulled out a typewriter, and then unearthed a sheaf of paper. In two minutes flat, the typewriter was on the card table and Miss Maryjane was typing up a contract between Timeless Films and Mr. Elvis Presley for a two-picture deal based on scripts to be agreed upon later. At the bottom, she typed her name and his with spaces for their signatures. She whipped out the paper and presented it to Elvis.

"Looks good," Elvis said. "We can work out the fees and points and stuff like that later. Got a pen?"

Aronson reached inside her blazer and produced a Parker fountain pen. Elvis removed the cap and placed the contract on the table in front of him. He raised the pen, then halted.

"Of course, to make it legal and all, money's got to exchange hands," Elvis said. "My daddy taught me that."

Aronson looked up at him apprehensively. "How much did you have in mind?"

"Oh, just a token, ma'am, so it looks serious. Say five hundred dollars? Cash, of course, so it's a done deal right here and now."

Bait and switch.

Aronson didn't hesitate for a second. She had oh so cleverly gotten everything she wanted. *The movie deal of a lifetime.* She walked briskly to the safe and kneeled down in front of it, Elvis following soundlessly behind her. She twirled the combination lock forward and back and forward again, then pressed down on the handle and swung the door open.

She was reaching for the steel money box on the bottom shelf when Elvis clamped one arm around her neck and cupped his other hand over her mouth. Aronson squirmed. She tried to bite Elvis's hand. She shot one sharp elbow into his ribs, then the other. Elvis held tight.

A black notebook sat on the top shelf of the safe, smart snakeskin with a golden clasp like a teenager's diary. And next to it was a large manila envelope with the words E.P. NEGATIVES printed on it. Miss Maryjane Aronson's fortune. A two-blackmail deal.

24
LOOK UNDER *C*

WHAT would Mamma say? Putting a woman in a choke hold, robbing her, wrapping her up in duct tape that some workman left behind, and then setting her on top of that big brass safe like some kind of mummified hood ornament?

Not a gentlemanly thing to do, no ma'am. But then again, Miss Maryjane wasn't exactly a lady either. She was something else altogether, neither Madonna nor whore. She was the devil herself.

"Got what I needed," Elvis crooned to Murphy as he sauntered out of the building. "Next stop, UCLA labs."

Elvis considered slipping back into the Corvair's luggage compartment—he was still a wanted man, maybe even more so now—but at this moment he needed more light than the luggage compartment would afford him. As a compromise, he pulled on Murphy's white parachute-cloth parka, lacing the hood tight over his head and forehead, and settled into the passenger seat. He glanced at himself in the rearview mirror: the hood revealed a perfect puny circle of face. He looked like a plastic kewpie doll, the boobie prize at a county fair's weight-guessing booth. He looked nothing at all like a rock 'n' roll legend. Yup, the line between beauty and beast was a narrow one, all right.

"You got the names?" Murphy asked excitedly as he pulled into traffic.

"Think so," Elvis replied, waving the black snakeskin address book. Actually, he *knew* so: he'd taken a quick peek on the elevator ride down. Just at the *A*s. Maryjane's clients were listed alphabetically by last name only, followed by a phone number, then one, two, or three women's first names in parentheses—their favorite call girls, he figured—and finally some kind of code in capital letters—DOM and WHP and the like, whatever the heck they meant. Elvis had only recognized one of the A last names—a top lyricist at one of the major Hollywood song mills, a steady customer who specialized in sappy romantic ballads.

"So read to me, Elvis!" Murphy exclaimed. "My mouth is watering like a geyser over here."

Elvis opened the address book, then quickly closed it again. In the elevator, he had been unable to make himself peer inside the manila envelope that he'd also extracted from Aronson's safe. He was afraid that it would not contain what he hoped it would. And even if it did, he was loathe to look at those sickening photographs again. Now, he bit down on his lower lip and unclasped the envelope. Photo negatives, all right. Four strips of them. He pulled them out. Turning his back to Murphy, he held a strip up against the side window. They were rolling past the evenly spaced street lights of Ventura Boulevard, and the negative images popped on and off, Elvis and Ann-Margret in stop action like a Charlie Chaplin reel. Pornographic slapstick.

"You got a match?" Elvis said.

Murphy reached into his shirt pocket, pulled out a book of matches, and handed them over to Elvis, who reached behind his back to take them.

"Thought you didn't smoke," Murphy said.

"Don't," Elvis said. "Bad habit."

He lit a match and ignited a corner of the strip of negatives. It burst immediately into a blue flame, licking right up to Elvis's fingertips and suffusing the car with putrid chemical smoke.

"Jesus, man! What the hell are you doing?" Murphy hollered.

Elvis rolled down the window with his left hand, still clutching the flaming negatives with his right. It burned the flesh on the first two digits of his thumb and forefinger, but Elvis held on. The pain felt right. *Cleansing.*

"You know that expression, 'burning with shame'?" Elvis said.

"Stop that!" Murphy shouted.

"That's what I'm doing, Murph. Burning with shame."

Elvis lit the second strip with the first, holding this one in his left hand and letting it burn right up to his fingertips again. Then the third and the fourth, the final strip of negatives. Despite the open window, the car now reeked with smoke. Murphy was coughing and sputtering and swearing at Elvis whenever he caught his breath, but Elvis was smiling, laughing, and now singing at the top of his lungs, improvising: "I just might turn into smoke, but I feel fine. I'm just a hunk, a hunk of burning shame." Now *there* was a darned good idea for a song.

"You're a crazy man," Murphy yelped. "Absolutely crazy."

"That's the truth, Murph," Elvis said. "You put that in our book too. Elvis Presley is crazy as a coot."

"Whatever you say, Elvis, but first read me *that* book." Murphy gestured at the black notebook.

Elvis opened the address book at random. The *R*s. First listing, "Radino, 386-3435, (Doris, Virginia)—DOM" Didn't ring any bells, although Murphy would probably know who it was. After all, that was a reporter's business—names and faces. Elvis was just about to say "Radino" out loud when he stopped himself. It just didn't feel right. This Radino probably had a wife. Kids too. A good job he worked hard at. Wouldn't be a surprise if he went to church too, just like those rich Frenchmen with a wife and a concubine that Regis had told him about. He was a lying man and a cheating man, but was that anybody's business but his own? It was just like those pictures of him and Miss Ann. Nobody's business.

But one of these names was not just a lying and cheating man, he was a murderer. Holly's murderer. The man who set up Squirm Littlejon. That's what getting ahold of this notebook was all about. Elvis flipped through the pages with his scorched thumb. There were easily a hundred names in there, maybe more. Miss Mary-jane hadn't put a little star next to one of them to indicate *this one here, he's the murderer*. What the devil had Elvis expected?

At the very least he could check for the names of people he suspected. He flipped to the *L*s, scanned down the list, then up again. No LeFevre; it wasn't Wayne. Next the *F*s. No Ned Florbid. The *G*s. Not even Mickey Grieves was in here. Of course, Mickey had worked out his own personal arrangement with Holly—rent in trade; he hadn't needed Miss Maryjane's scheduling services.

Man, Elvis was no closer to figuring this thing out than he was a week ago. The only difference is that now the police were looking for *him*. And all that running around catching teardrops was a joke too. Hector Garcia had a mere dozen DNA samples to match with Holly's last customer and most of those were stunt-men, not Hollywood bigwigs who could bankroll Aronson's new studio. Who was Elvis kidding? He wasn't a detective, he was just a fool trying to outrun his own pent-up teardrops.

Mike Murphy was peering over Elvis's shoulder.

"Look under *C*," he said softly.

"What for?"

"Just look."

ELVIS could hear Dolores Suarez's heart-rending wail from the laboratory corridor. With Murphy panting behind him, he jogged to the lab door and opened it.

Delores was on her knees, bent over, her face in her hands. She was crying uncontrollably, gasping for air, now wailing again, her thin shoulders quaking under her white laboratory coat. Hector stood over her, hopelessly attempting to comfort her by patting her head. Regis was nowhere to be seen.

"What happened?" Elvis.

Hector shook his head sadly, said nothing.

"Where's Regis?"

Hector shrugged miserably. Delores let out a heart-breaking moan.

Elvis swiftly approached them, dropped to his knees in front of Delores. He reached out a hand and touched the side of the woman's face. Her salty tears stung his burnt fingertips.

"I'm sorry, ma'am," he said softly. "Whatever it is, I'm real sorry."

"Re . . . Regis," she stammered, but she could not go on.

Elvis gazed up at Hector beseechingly.

"I . . . I checked her results," Hector said haltingly. "Twice. Starting from scratch each time. But always the same. No mistake."

Elvis nodded. He was pretty sure he knew what was coming.

"Delores took a cell sample from Regis too," Hector went on. "A strand of his hair."

"He . . . He made a joke when I did it," Delores said, crying more softly now, a painful smile on her fine oval face. "He said, 'If I go bald, it is your fault.'"

"We needed it for elimination, of course," Hector continued. "Like with yours. In case you had contaminated the other samples by handling them. A double check. We had no other reason to take it."

"I understand," Elvis said.

"It matched," Hector blurted. "Regis's DNA and the last man who was with Holly McDougal. The murderer. A perfect match."

"Jesus Christ, it is Regis!" Murphy exploded.

"No. I . . . I . . . didn't know. He . . . He never told me," Delores stammered. She began bawling full out again. "I spoke too soon!" she wailed.

"She accused him," Hector said softly.

"I said to him, 'How could you do this to me? How could you put the proof right in front of my eyes? *My* eyes! Why *mine*?" Delores sobbed.

"I did not realize immediately either," Hector said. "I had forgotten that Regis has an identical twin."

"What the hell difference does that make?" Murphy asked vehemently.

"An identical twin has identical DNA," Elvis said. "Same blueprint, same calling card."

"My God!" Murphy cried.

"That is true, of course," Hector said. "But already, Regis, he had run."

"Where did he go?"

Hector shrugged.

"He went to his brother's," Murphy blurted. "To LeRoy's. I bet he's there already."

"You got to be right," Elvis said. He rocked back up onto his feet, then leaned over and kissed the top of Dr. Suarez's head. "I'll go get him for you. It's going to be all right, Miss Delores. I promise you."

Mike Murphy knew precisely where California Supreme Court Justice LeRoy Clifford lived. He also knew the home address of every other State Supreme Court justice, not to mention of every DA and police commissioner; he said a "mental phone book" was what separated the reporters who got scoops from the lugs who ended up covering night court their entire lives.

Justice Clifford lived in Beverly Hills in a twenty-eight-room estate wedged capaciously between the mansions of Dick Powell and Phil Silver; his Alpine Drive address was accompanied by a rare asterisk for "Not Worth Looking At" on those star maps that celebrity-struck tourists dutifully followed. Murph also knew that Judge LeRoy was married to one Miranda Kurtz, a grapefruit heiress from Palm Beach, that they had two children and went to church every Sunday at St. Brigit's Celtic Christian Ministries in Costa Mesa. In other words, according to Regis's profile, LeRoy was just the kind of upstanding citizen who liked a little something strange on the side.

"Clifford" was the third entry under *C* in Maryjane Aronson's little black book: "Clifford, 555-9468, (Holly)—LO."

"Holy God!" Elvis had exclaimed. But then he had angrily swung around to Murphy and demanded, "How the hell did you know?"

"I didn't," Murphy had replied. "Just a hunch. The jewelry in Holly's safety deposit box was insured by the Clifford estate. At least, most of it was. Family heirlooms. My jeweler friend recognized it immediately."

"But it can't be Regis!"

"I hope to God you're right, Elvis."

"I know I'm right."

Murphy was now turning off Santa Monica Boulevard onto Alpine Drive. Elvis loosened the tie-string on the parka hood, then pulled off the entire parka. He was making an unexpected social call in Beverly Hills; for the first time today, it was going to be an advantage to be unmistakably Elvis Presley.

There was a gate and a guard in front of the palatial home of Justice and Mrs. LeRoy Clifford. Through the gate, Elvis could see a half-dozen limousines lined up in front of the main entrance. Apparently the Cliffords were entertaining. Murphy stopped for inspection, rolling down his window.

"Your name, please?" the guard asked imperiously. He was wearing the police-like garb of a private security agency, but he carried himself like a Buckingham sentry.

Elvis leaned over Murphy and looked up at the guard. "Presley," he said. "Elvis Aron."

"Are you expected, Mr. Presley?" the guard said, not blinking an eye.

"I'm the evening's entertainment," Elvis replied, deadpan.

The guard responded with a patronizing smile that said, "So, Elvis, isn't it a long way down?" and then opened the gates and waved them through.

They parked in front of the lead limousine, directly under the portico. This was undoubtedly against the house rules, but neither Murphy nor Elvis were feeling especially rule-abiding at the moment. A butler in a monkey suit met them at the front door. He, at least, seemed more impressed than the gate guard with the evening's entertainment. He immediately summoned the lady of the house.

Miranda Kurtz Clifford was a painfully thin and angular woman with overbred pinched features and pale blue eyes that looked as if they had spent a lifetime trying to hide her shyness. She was wearing a lavender silk gown that dipped where her cleavage should have been and a massive diamond necklace hung from her birdlike neck like an albatross; she obviously knew that the forty-carat diamonds were the secret of her attraction. Elvis could not help automatically comparing her with the image of Holly McDougal shimmying on that Moviola screen.

"Goodness me, another surprise guest!" Miss Miranda gushed. "It's an honor, Mr. Presley. I'm a big fan, you know, although I don't tell anybody that."

"Your secret's safe with me, ma'am," Elvis said. "This here is Mike Murphy, my biographer."

Mrs. Clifford shook each man's hand. "The judge loves his surprises. He didn't tell me that you—"

"Oh, we aren't expected, Mrs. Clifford," Elvis said. "It's just a friend of mine told me to meet him here. The judge's brother, Regis." Miranda Clifford's aqua eyes turned even paler. Her well-orchestrated dinner party was not going according to plan, and clearly this was a woman who depended heavily on plans, probably for every waking moment of her day.

"They . . . The judge asked not to be disturbed," Mrs. Clifford blurted. She forced another inbred gracious smile. "He said they would only be a couple moments."

"Him and Regis," Elvis said.

The judge's wife hesitated. "Yes," she said finally. "They haven't seen each other in years, you know."

"I know, Mrs. Clifford. Must be very emotional for them," Elvis said. "Where are they?"

Mrs. Clifford looked utterly distraught. She was a hostess dedicated to her guests' gratifications, but she was also a woman who unquestioningly obeyed her husband's instructions; he was, after all, the Judge.

"It's his medication," Murphy suddenly piped in. "Regis's insulin. He left it behind. If he doesn't take it soon . . ."

Elvis nodded gravely. That Murphy sure was a gifted story-teller. "My goodness, I . . . I didn't realize—" the hostess sputtered.

"No way you could know, ma'am," Elvis said. "Why don't you just point the way. I bet your guests are waiting for you."

It was probably that last that nailed it, the reminder that Miss Miranda's guests might be feeling neglected. She pointed up the long curved staircase. "The judge's study. It's in the back."

"Thank you, Mrs. Clifford," Elvis said.

"You're quite welcome," she replied.

Elvis was on the first step when Miss Miranda called to him. "It wouldn't be any trouble at all to set extra places for you and Mr. Murphy," she said.

"You're very kind," Elvis said. "Why don't we just play it by ear, okay?"

"Of course, 'by ear,'" she trilled, as if "playing it by ear" was the most daring concept she had entertained in years.

Elvis continued up the staircase, Murphy a step behind him. At the landing, they tiptoed on the carpet runner toward the rear of the house.

"I don't know who you are anymore." Regis's voice coming through the half-open door of the study. Or was it LeRoy's? Their voices would be identical too, wouldn't they? Everything the same.

"I don't know what you are talking about. I have remained the same, unlike you."

"The same? You mean you've always lived liked this? A double life? One holier-than-thou and the other in the gutter?"

"The gutter?" An ugly laugh. "Do not speak to me of the gutter, Regis. I, at least, have never woken up in one."

Elvis pressed himself against the wall, slowly sidled up to the hinged side of the door jamb, signaling Murphy to halt behind him. From this angle, Elvis could only see one of the men; he was standing in profile against floor-to-ceiling brown velvet drapes, his arms straight at his sides. Feature by feature, it was Regis's face—the jutting chin, the long straight nose, the ironically lifted eyebrow. But this man was wearing a well-tailored and well-pressed black suit, gold cuff-links, a red silk tie. *LeRoy.* The *successful* twin. The *good* twin. At that moment, LeRoy made a half-turn and Elvis jumped back, but not before he had seen the black eye patch and scar-rutted skin below it where LeRoy's face went in where it should have gone out.

"I can understand all of it, LeRoy. Really, I can. The women—"

"Not women, Regis—woman. *Just Holly.* She was the only one."

"In all those years?"

"In all those years, she was the only one I wanted."

"For God's sake, she was just a child."

"Not in the way she made me feel." A long pause. Elvis edged back to where he could peer inside the study. This time he could see only Regis. He was standing perfectly straight, but his hands were clenched. He was trembling. "*That* is one thing you could never understand, Regis. How that girl made me feel."

"You loved her."

"Yes." Not DOM or WHP after LeRoy's name in Aronson's black book; just LO—for "Love."

"I can understand that, LeRoy. I have loved a woman. I . . . I love one now."

"No! You do not understand what it is for me to love a woman. A beautiful woman. A sexy woman. That does not happen to me. For other men, yes. But not me. Not with this."

Elvis could not see LeRoy, but he realized he must have been pointing at his own face. Regis bowed his head, stuffed both his trembling hands into his jacket pockets. "But you loved Holly McDougal," he said.

"Yes. She did not love me, of course. But that did not matter. I didn't need that too. Having her was enough. Even sharing her with God knows how many other men did not matter."

Another long pause. From downstairs, a sudden burst of tinny laughter. One of Judge Clifford's dinner guests must have gotten off a witty one.

"It was heaven, Regis." LeRoy continued. "Heaven on earth for a few hours each week. But those few hours saturated me. It was like a transfusion. She changed me, changed me into another man. A whole man."

"You should have gone with her. Married her," Regis said.

"And then what, Regis?" That ugly laugh again. Bitter—the hollow sound of that sunken cheekbone. "Lived happily ever after? On what? I would have lost my seat on the court. Lost my house. Lost everything and everybody. The Cliffords have endured enough shame already."

Regis put a hand to his forehead, rubbed it. Of course he, himself, was the shame that the Cliffords had endured already.

"But you loved her," Regis said.

"Yes. For a few hours every week. That was all I needed."

"And you had that."

"Yes, I had that."

"What went wrong, LeRoy?"

"Holly. Holly went wrong."

LeRoy suddenly appeared in Elvis's view, pacing deliberately toward Regis. His right elbow was crooked and in his right hand was a pistol, a World War One German Luger. He was pointing it at his twin brother. He must have been pointing the gun at him the entire time.

Elvis sucked in his breath. There were a good twenty feet between him and LeRoy. If Elvis ran at him, dived and tackled him, LeRoy would easily have enough time to get off at least one shot at Regis. And one shot is all it would take.

"How? How did she go wrong?" Regis asked.

"She got greedy. She wanted more, always more. More money, more jewelry. Mother's jewelry. Her necklaces."

"I wondered if those were Mother's."

"What? If what were Mother's?" LeRoy straightened his arm, jutting the pistol within inches of his brother's chest. Regis stood perfectly straight, perfectly still. His trembling had stopped altogether. If he was fast, he could slap the gun to the side, then knee LeRoy in the groin and subdue him. But it was obvious that Regis was going to do no such thing. He was his brother's captive, his victim, and Regis just stood there with defiant calm, as if he had been longing for this moment since the Clifford twins had been fooling around with a BB gun by the side of the lake, thirty years ago.

"The jewelry in Holly's bank box," Regis said. "I thought it looked familiar, but it didn't seem possible."

"Her bank box?"

"Yes. Holly's sister told me about it. And Elvis talked his way into access to it."

"Oh yes, your friend, Elvis!" LeRoy snarled, thumping the barrel of the Luger against Regis's chest. "The pea-brain warbler. My brother's big-time Hollywood pal!"

"You have no idea who that man is, what is in his soul," Regis said.

The barrel of a loaded gun was pressed against his chest directly over his heart, and Regis was defending Elvis as if he were his brother. Elvis's own heart swelled.

"You must have run out of Mother's jewelry eventually," Regis went on.

"Yes, I ran out, although Holly didn't believe me at first. So I bought more jewelry, new jewelry, expensive jewelry."

"Because you loved her," Regis said sympathetically.

"Yes, because I loved her." LeRoy took a long breath. "And then because she threatened me."

LeRoy's misshapen face knotted into a grotesque grimace. For a moment, he absently spread his arms in a gesture of futility and defeat, and with this gesture the gun pointed away from Regis toward the ceiling. Elvis swung silently into the doorway, desperately trying to catch Regis's eye. "Now!" he mouthed. "Grab the gun now!"

But Regis did not see him. And he did not move. Instead, he gazed directly into his twin brother's eye as if warning him, as if reminding LeRoy to point the gun back at him. Elvis pulled back out of sight again.

"Did she threaten to expose you?" Regis asked. "To tell the world that Judge LeRoy Clifford was cheating on his wife with a teenage girl?"

LeRoy nodded. He appeared to be struggling to control his arm, to aim the gun at Regis again.

"And so when there was nothing else left, you had to kill her," Regis said matter-of-factly.

"Holly wanted to be a star," LeRoy answered in a monotone. "A movie star. She knew about the new studio Maryjane Aronson was planning to start. Knew that I was part of it, that I was arranging the financing."

"With your friends," Regis said.

"With my colleagues." LeRoy offered his brother a bitterly ironic, lopsided smile. "My colleagues on Maryjane's client list."

"And Holly wanted to star in Aronson's films."

"Yes," LeRoy said. "She said that is how Marilyn Monroe got her start. That one day she was just a bit player, and the next she was a movie star. Holly didn't see why it should be any different for her."

"But Aronson didn't agree," Regis said.

"Aronson laughed in my face when I suggested it. She said Holly was a nothing. She couldn't carry a film in a million years. That she simply did not have star power. That she had risen as high as she would ever get professionally."

"To the level of a call girl," Regis said.

LeRoy's arm rose, stiffened. Now the gun was again pressing against his brother's chest. Elvis cringed. He should have made a run at LeRoy when he had the chance.

"I could have killed her," LeRoy snarled. "Killed Aronson when she said that."

"But you didn't. And when you told Holly that you were not going to be able to get her name in lights, she threatened you again."

"Yes."

"And that is when you killed her. Strangled her," Regis said.

LeRoy shoved hard with the gun barrel. Regis stumbled backward, but remained on his feet. He stood straight and immobile again, waiting for his brother.

"It wasn't even the threat of exposure at that point," LeRoy said quietly. "She said she would never be with me again. Never make love to me again. She . . . she said that at least she would never have to see my disgusting face on top of her again."

And then Judge LeRoy Clifford closed his one eye, shut it tight against the humiliation of sight itself.

Elvis jumped into the doorway and charged at LeRoy. "Grab the gun! *Now*, Regis!"

Regis's head spun around. He leapt between Elvis and his brother.

"No!" he screamed savagely. *"HE'S MY BROTHER!"*

LeRoy's eye snapped open. He raised the pistol, then stuffed the barrel into his own mouth. Regis grabbed his arm, yanked it away. The gun fired and Regis fell backward, his knees crumbling under him.

Elvis dove at LeRoy's feet. But it was too late. LeRoy had crammed the barrel back into his mouth and the gun fired for a second time. LeRoy blew out the left side of his face, the "good" side, and catapulted backward onto his back, dead.

Elvis crawled to Regis. Blood gushed from Regis's chest, but he was conscious.

"Leroy?" Regis whimpered.

Tears flooded Elvis's eyes as he gazed down at the surviving twin.

"It's your turn now," Elvis whispered.

26
TOO HUMAN

THE sun was rising in Beverly Hills when Elvis and Murphy finally drove away from the Clifford estate.

The police and an ambulance had arrived at the same time. Regis had been taken off to Cedars Hospital; the medic said that the bullet had missed his aorta by only inches, but his life was not in any danger. Elvis had been certain that the police would take him into custody and the prospect didn't disturb him in the least. He had found out what he had set out to discover; he did not need to hide from anyone any longer. But it turned out that Jilly-Jo Cathcart had heard that the police were looking for Elvis in connection with Grieves's murder. She had gone to the Maywood police station that afternoon to give a statement about everything that had happened in the stunt shack that morning. At the Clifford residence, the police said that they only wanted Elvis to drop by later and give his own statement to corroborate the circumstances of the freak accident that had cost Mickey Grieves his life.

Miranda Clifford had remained eerily calm when informed that her husband was dead, his life taken by his own hand. Her guests were eager to leave her aborted dinner party as quickly as possible lest the press corps arrive and snap their pictures amid this messy scene. The police, ever sensitive to the wealthy's needs, permitted them to do so, Miss Miranda courteously gathering their wraps for them.

Murphy had done most of the talking to the police. In his fine reporter's mind, he had recorded every word spoken, every movement, every shot fired. When he finished, he had implored the law officers to protect his statement from the eyes of any prying journalists, "For obvious legal reasons," he had explained to them, although everyone knew full well that he was protecting his own scoop. And now he and Elvis were racing to the *L.A. Times* in Mike Murphy's Corvair. There was still time to make the afternoon edition.

Neither Elvis nor Murphy spoke. Elvis stared out the side window watching the mansions of the Hollywood elite slip by. There were still many unanswered questions—about Aronson and Grieves and Warden Reardon—but he was not thinking about any of these now. Elvis was thinking about LeRoy Clifford and Holly McDougal and the mysterious forces that joined a man and a woman, about the ballads of passionate love that never would be written and sung, that never *could* be written and sung because they were too true, too *human*.

"Jesus! Behind us!" Murphy said.

Elvis turned, gaped out through the car's rear window. The blue Beetle. At not quite four in the morning on Santa Monica Boulevard in Beverly Hills, the grizzled man in the nightwatch cap was a car's length behind them, frantically waving his garish-colored box in the air outside the driver's window.

Murphy yanked the car to the shoulder, screeched to a halt. The Beetle tore by them on the left, then swerved onto the shoulder and stopped twenty feet ahead of them. Elvis and Murphy jumped out of their car and ran in tandem toward the Beetle.

Elvis grabbed the door handle on the driver's side, yanked it open, wrenched the driver out of his seat by the back of his neck, spun him around, and put him in a full-Nelson over the hood.

"At last," the old guy in the knit cap murmured, smiling painfully.

"Who the devil are you?" Elvis barked.

"Just a fisherman," the man replied happily. "A fisherman with the best damned script you'll ever read in your life!"

He gestured at the cardboard box with the gleaming, blood-red skull and crossbones painted on its cover that sat on his car seat. Murphy reached in and picked it up. Elvis released his hold on the man, took the box from Murphy, and lifted off the cover. The title page read:

Blue Suede Cruise
by Captain Tim Timmons
The True Story of the Singing Fisherman

The only other vehicle on Santa Monica Boulevard at that hour was a farm truck carrying fifty crates of apricots up from Littlerock. Looking out his window, the driver of that pick-up would have seen three men standing by the side of the road, one bearded, one bald, and one who looked for all the world like Elvis Presley. And the bald one and the Elvis-looking fellow were laughing so uproariously, so crazily, so infectiously, that that farm truck driver couldn't have helped bursting into laughter too.

ELVIS was sleeping in his own bed for the first time in a week when the phone rang. He blinked open his eyes, raised himself onto his elbows, and squinted over at his bed-table clock. It was ten in the morning. He picked up the phone.

"Yup," he said into the mouthpiece.

"Hey, Elvis. I just realized you might be still sleeping over there. Want me to ring back later?"

"Who is this?"

"Me, Squirm."

"Squirm?" Elvis finished waking up real fast. "Where the heck are you?"

"Rome," Squirm said. "Rome, Italy. It's awful nice here too. Sunny, but not *too* sunny, you know?"

"How the devil did you get to Rome?"

"The long way," Squirm said, chuckling. "By way of Costa Rica and Marrakesh, actually. Gotta be a faster way, I'm sure."

Elvis sat up straight in his bed.

"Slow down, Squirm," he said. "I'm a few hours behind you."

"We got the *International Herald* this morning," Littlejon said. "The whole story about Clifford's brother and Holly and that Aronson woman. Nancy never trusted her, you know."

"Oh," was all Elvis could manage at that particular moment. "Anyway," Squirm went on, "We figured it was okay to call now, the coast being clear and all. I mean, I wanted to call earlier, but you never know who's listening, do you?"

"No," Elvis said. He tried shaking his head vigorously to get his brain fully engaged.

"Well, like they say, all's well that ends well," Squirm continued cheerfully. "I already landed a job here. Gernario Films. Spaghetti westerns. They need a little American know-how in the stunt department. And like I was just saying to Nancy, I owe it all to you. Every bit of it. You gave me my life back, Elvis, and I will never forget that as long as I—"

"Hold on, a minute. *Nancy?* You were just saying to *Nancy*! Nancy Pollard?"

"Yeah, that's the best part, Elvis. She's here with me. Flew over yesterday. We got a lot of time to make up for."

"I, uh, I bet you do, Squirm," Elvis said.

"And listen, Elvis? How's that ankle of yours doing? I felt real bad about that, you know."

"Just fine, Squirm. Healed itself." It actually was healed, Elvis had realized the night before.

"That's terrific," Squirm Littlejon said. "I got a few twists and bruises myself along the way. Man, I did some stunts out there, the stunts of a lifetime. Especially that one where I slid down the heating duct of the prison infirmary."

"What?"

"The heating ducts. Narrow as a drain pipe, but that didn't keep *el bandito diminuto* from squirming through."

"Reardon showed you—?"

"Reardon didn't show me dip for diddle. I'd been planning this escape for years. But seeing how much you believed in me finally gave me the gumption to do it. I had some real close calls, I'll tell you, but you saved my ass when you put out the word for nobody to shoot at me." Squirm laughed. "Well, Nancy's waiting on me, so I got to go. You know how women are, Elvis."

Not really, Elvis thought. In fact, not at all.

"You take care, Squirm," Elvis said and he hung up. He got out of bed and headed down to the kitchen, his head spinning. Unbelievable. Neither Reardon nor LeRoy nor anybody else had set up Squirm's escape; it was all his own doing. But even more incredible was the fact that Nancy Pollard, the woman who had helped put Squirm away for life, was now with him in Rome to pick up their romance where it had left off. No sense in Elvis even *trying* to get his mind around that one. He put up the kettle for coffee.

Regis and Delores were a different story; their feelings of forgiveness and love made perfect sense to him. When Elvis had visited Regis at the hospital yesterday, Delores was at his side, lovingly stroking his head. His bullet wound was healing, but the wound in his heart over his late brother would never heal completely, Regis told Elvis. He was wrong about the gratifications of revenge, he said. Dead wrong. Revenge was puny stuff when compared to brotherly love.

Delores was going to wait for Regis to get out of the hospital, and then the two of them would fly to Santa Teresa together, Regis to remain there. He was thinking of studying up on Mexican patent law so he could patent the discoveries that Hector and Delores were making in their laboratory. Regis and Delores planned to get married down there as soon as possible and hoped that Elvis would come for the ceremony. "No excuses," Regis had said, managing a smile. "After all, you've got a fresh passport."

Delores had accompanied Elvis out to the hospital corridor. There, she had suddenly presented him with a record album, the Spanish one he'd seen in El Disco Norde's window entitled, *Rubias, Morenas Y Pelirrojas*. Delores wanted him to autograph it for her mother. Elvis obliged, writing to Señora Suarez that her daughter was going to make his friend, Regis, one fine wife. Handing the album back, Elvis confessed that he didn't really know what "Rubias, Morenas Y Pelirrojas" meant.

Delores had laughed. "It means, 'Blondes, Brunettes, and Redheads,'" she said.

Elvis looked at her quizzically.

"It's the name we gave to your movie, *It Happened at the World's Fair*," she said.

Maybe once in a while, a title gained something in translation. There was only one decent song in *World's Fair* that Elvis could remember, the one called "Happy Ending."

The kettle was boiling. Elvis made himself a mug of Maxwell House instant, ladling in four spoonfuls of sugar, and then sat down at the kitchen table. Yesterday's *Los Angeles Times* still lay there with Mike Murphy's front-page article as the second lead. This was the article that had found its way into the *International Herald Tribune*, along with hundreds of other newspapers across the country. It picked up where Murphy's scoop in the afternoon edition had left off, with the story of Justice LeRoy Clifford's suicide. Elvis glanced down at it.

Judge's Suicide Linked to Murder Cover-Up
Studio Head and Stuntman Incriminated

Studio City, Nov. 21. When State Supreme Court Justice LeRoy Clifford took his own life at his estate yesterday, he not only left behind a tangled web of love, betrayal, and murder, but a cover-up of that murder which involved Miss Maryjane Aronson, CEO of the newly incorporated, Timeless Films, and Mr. Michael Grieves, a former MGM stuntman who coincidently died in a freak accident on the MGM lot on Tuesday. . . .

Murphy had gathered the material for this follow-up story yesterday after dropping Elvis off at his house on Perugia Way. From Elvis's, Murphy had driven directly to the makeshift offices of Timeless Films in Studio City where he found the fledgling studio's CEO still enthroned on her open bronze safe swaddled in duct tape, wild eyed and reeking of fear and bodily fluids. Murphy had struck a deal with her: *Tell all and I will set you free.* Murphy had unwound the tape to Maryjane Aronson's neck, leaving the rest of her bound like a mummy as he sat down in front of her with his open notebook.

According to the *Times'* anonymous source, after Judge Clifford left the murder victim on the evening of March 20, 1960, he went directly to the office of Miss Aronson in the project development department of MGM. At this time, Clifford was still wearing the World War One army uniform that Aronson had procured for him from the studio wardrobe for his assignations with Miss McDougal. The outfit served as a disguise for Clifford; he always looked like just another extra on the studio lot, a gas mask completing his camouflage. . . .

Elvis realized that it must have been the same outfit LeRoy wore when he had threatened Connie Spinelli.

Miss Aronson waited until Judge Clifford had sufficient time to get home, then anonymously phoned the police, claiming that she had witnessed the stuntman, Fredrick Littlejon, leaving the scene of the crime. . . .

According to Aronson, it was just the luck of the draw that LeRoy had been selected by the chief DA to prosecute the case. Similarly, it had been only happenchance that Mickey Grieves recommended Regis as Littlejon's lawyer; Grieves had heard through the grapevine that Regis had a reputation for losing a high percentage of his cases.

As to Grieves's own role in the cover-up, from his lying testimony to his threat on Elvis to his cleverly contrived murder of Will Cathcart, Maryjane Aronson said that it was motivated by nothing less pathetic and banal than Aronson's promise to upgrade him from stuntman to speaking parts in Timeless Films's motion pictures. Like everyone else, Mickey Grieves had dreamed of making it big in Hollywood.

The other stuntmen who testified that they had never had sex with Holly McDougal were simply protecting themselves from recriminations by their wives and girlfriends. Grieves had convinced them that Squirm was unquestionably the murderer and that they had nothing to gain by sullying their own good names. This, it seems, was the insignificant piece of information that Will Cathcart had heard from his colleagues and that had ultimately cost him his life.

Finally, it turned out that Supreme Court Justice Clifford had not confessed the entire truth to his brother. Holly McDougal may have been the only woman in Aronson's stable of call girls who he ever loved, but not the only one he'd ever slept with. Judge LeRoy had been a steady customer of Aronson's for years, which accounted for his long-standing position as the behind-the-scenes financial consultant and deal-maker for Aronson's film ambitions.

At the time of Clifford's suicide, Maryjane Aronson was president and chief executive officer of a new studio, Timeless Films, Inc., whose first film, a remake of *Rebel Without a Cause*, was expected to lens early next year. Judge Clifford was a silent partner with twenty-five percent equity in Timeless.

After Mike Murphy had taken down every word, he had left Maryjane Aronson bound and perched on the safe while he phoned Elvis. He told Elvis the whole story, then asked if he actually should let her go.

"Your call, Elvis," Murphy had said.

Elvis had not answered for several minutes. LeRoy Clifford was dead, Mickey Grieves also, both of their debts to society paid up in full, if such a transaction was actually possible. Squirm Littlejon was exonerated and free, which is really all Elvis had wanted in the first place.

But there was something else to consider: Murphy had made no mention of Aronson's blackmail photographs of Elvis and Ann-Margret. Apparently, she had said nothing about them. At this point, it was the only secret left unexposed.

"Let her go," Elvis had said.

Maryjane Aronson was on a plane for foreign parts unknown by the time Murphy's story hit the newsstands in that evening's *Times*.

Elvis took his coffee out onto the patio and was slowly sipping it when the phone rang again. It was the Colonel.

"Pick you up for the press conference in half an hour," Parker said.

"I'll be ready," Elvis answered. There wasn't really much to say to the press now that Murphy's story was out, but Parker had convinced Elvis that it would be a good idea to make a public appearance after all the rumors that had been circulating about him this past week. "Just to reassure your fans," Parker had said.

"Listen, I've got a little surprise cooked up for our pals in the press corps," Parker was now saying excitedly. "Our new picture. Allied Artists. Seven hundred and fifty thousand up front and fifty percent of profits. Incredible deal, Elvis. Unheard of. Nobody makes deals like I do."

"What kind of picture, Tom?"

"Wonderful script, son. You're going to love it," Parker said. "Listen to this: it's called *Tickle Me*. And it's got 'Elvis' written all over it."

Elvis flinched, but at this moment he was too weary to argue about anything. He went back upstairs, dressed for the press conference, came back down again, and then stood motionlessly at the front window, gazing out at the palm-lined avenue. It looked so peaceful out there, peaceful and domestic. It made Elvis long for home, his *real* home. Elvis hadn't spoken to Priscilla since she'd returned to Graceland. She had phoned several times this past week, Joanie had told him. He really ought to call her. Maybe after the press conference, call her up and tell her he was coming right home.

Suddenly, a bright-yellow Oldsmobile convertible came into view and lurched to a stop in front of his house. A young woman jumped out of the car and came running toward his front door, her flaming red hair streaming behind her. It was Ann-Margret and she was bawling. Man, he was definitely not in the mood for a hysterical woman just now. He reluctantly opened the door and looked at her. Golly, Miss Ann surely was one fine-looking woman.

"He's dead!" she cried.

"What?" Elvis's heart accelerated. "Who's dead *now*?"

"The President," Miss Ann moaned. "He's been shot. In Dallas."

"President Kennedy?"

"Yes!"

"Oh Lord! Who did it?"

"They don't know," Ann-Margret sobbed. *"They don't know."*

Elvis threw his arm around her and guided her to a sofa. He turned on the television set and sat down beside her, trembling himself now, tears flooding from his eyes. Behind them, the phone began ringing. Elvis reached into his pocket for his bottle of painkillers.

THE END

KINDRED SPIRITS . . .

Why not join the

DEAN STREET PRESS
FACEBOOK GROUP

for lively bookish chat
and more

Scan the QR code below

Or follow this link
**www.facebook.com/groups/
deanstreetpress**

Made in the USA
Middletown, DE
17 October 2023